2 ot

1499
9

D0379288

Praise for
The BOY DETECTIVE

"The book is rich with recollections and with the lush wanderings of memory and imagination. In combination they draw the reader into one of the most entertaining, thoughtful and deeply moving minds among nonfiction writers today. . . . The boy detective chases suspects and finds clues all over his city. The adult writer asks the question 'How do you walk in the world?' and answers it partly with a line from Wallace Stevens—'I was the world in which I walked'—but mainly with this quiet, triumphant ambulation, a characteristically eloquent and multiply rewarding book."
                                                —*Washington Post*

"Roger Rosenblatt's evocative memoir, *The Boy Detective,* also challenges easy categorization. His book combines a walking tour around vanished Manhattan with a meditation, not only on the classic mystery fiction he loves, but also on those larger metaphysical mysteries that defy even the shrewdest detective's reasoning."
                                                —NPR's *Fresh Air*

"That Roger Rosenblatt's *The Boy Detective* has no table of contents will make perfect sense to readers who follow the meandering path that constitutes his charming memoir of growing up around Gramercy Park. Categorizing his musings would be too confining." —*New York Times*

"Beautiful sentences spill out such as, 'Everyone dwells in one past or another, and to a greater or lesser extent, is ruled by it.' A hallmark of memoir is the self now reflecting on the self then. This book pulls off the high wire feat of illuminating that double identity and giving readers the mental atmospheres of both narrators, the rascal back then and the reflective adult today . . . deliciously satisfying." —*New York Journal of Books*

"In the vein of his other recent works, Rosenblatt (*Making Toast*) has taken memoir writing—a subject he teaches at State University of New York at Stony Brook—and turned it on its head once again. Walking the Manhattan streets of his childhood, Rosenblatt uses the city landscape to delve into eclectic ruminations on the nature of time and space, the slipperiness of reality and memory. By mixing in history, literary references, geography, philosophy, and poetry, he is somehow able to create a 14th Street where (or when) Luchow, a nineteenth-century restaurant, sits side by side with a modern Trader Joe's store. Rosenblatt's writing is honest, yet it produces a magical world unto itself." —*Publishers Weekly* (starred review)

"Funny, intelligent, page-turning, this memoir doesn't just describe a 1940s childhood in New York City; rather, it ruminates on the life of an artist born in and shaped by its streets. With its noirish, casual voice, this book is also, in a way, its own kind of mystery, although, the bodies and crimes are mostly metaphorical."

—Daily Beast

"With the beautiful, lyrical writing and thoughtful reflection for which he is known, Rosenblatt offers beautifully rendered memories of childhood and ongoing curiosity about the city he so obviously loves."

—*Booklist*

"Memoir, urban travelogue or summing up of a career grounded in the written word, Roger Rosenblatt's *The Boy Detective* is an elegant and wise journey through an incomparable city and a meaning-filled life."

—Shelf Awareness

"Readers who believe a journey is worth more than the destination will find a kindred spirit in Rosenblatt, who is generous company during his wanderings."

—*Christian Science Monitor*

ALSO BY
ROGER ROSENBLATT

The BOY DETECTIVE

A New York Childhood

ROGER ROSENBLATT

An Imprint of HarperCollins*Publishers*

Portions of this book have appeared, in different forms, in the *New Republic*, the *New York Times Book Review*, the *Washington Post*, and *Time* magazine.

THE BOY DETECTIVE. Copyright © 2013 by Roger Rosenblatt. All rights reserved. Printed in the United States of America. No part of this book may be used or reproduced in any manner whatsoever without written permission except in the case of brief quotations embodied in critical articles and reviews. For information address HarperCollins Publishers, 195 Broadway, New York, NY 10007.

HarperCollins books may be purchased for educational, business, or sales promotional use. For information please e-mail the Special Markets Department at SPsales@harpercollins.com.

A hardcover edition of this book was published in 2013 by Ecco, an imprint of HarperCollins Publishers.

FIRST ECCO PAPERBACK EDITION PUBLISHED 2014.

Designed by Suet Yee Chong

Library of Congress Cataloging-in-Publication Data has been applied for.

ISBN 978-0-06-227719-0

14 15 16 17 18 OV/RRD   10 9 8 7 6 5 4 3 2 1

for Peter and Judy,
friends for a lifetime

"My dear fellow," said Sherlock Holmes, as we sat on either side of the fire in his lodgings at Baker Street, "life is infinitely stranger than anything which the mind of man could invent. We would not dare to conceive the things which are really mere commonplaces of existence."

—ARTHUR CONAN DOYLE, "A CASE OF IDENTITY"

Not less because in purple I descended
The western day through what you called
The loneliest air, not less was I myself.

—WALLACE STEVENS, "TEA AT THE PALAZ OF HOON"

"Why do you have to go back?"
"It's not over yet."

—*HARPER*

IT WAS ICE, pal, I don't mind telling you. The revolver was ice. Since nine-year-olds didn't wear suit jackets, I had to carry it in a jury-rigged shoulder holster under my polo shirt, and the cap gun was ice against my chest. The look was that of a kid who had just snitched a mango from a fruit stand and was trying to conceal it. Nonetheless, I managed to maintain a grim, professional demeanor, lest my suspects spot any weakness and get the upper hand. I trailed them among the secret stores and wholesale houses of the neither-here-nor-there neighborhoods of downtown New York. Most of them hung around the Met Life Building, which looked innocuous enough, but clearly was teeming with crime. The business-men under my surveillance also looked harmless, to anyone but me. I trailed them at short distances—called "rough shad-owing" in the trade—making it easy for them to notice me, because if the killer did not know he was being followed, no one else would either. I saw myself as acting simultaneously in real time and in a film noir, so I was both tracking my quarry and watching myself do it. For his part, the killer, sensing danger, would turn around from time to time, confused and annoyed at being pursued by a kid with a mango in his shirt.

WHICH LEADS ME, as you might expect, to the unpleasantness at Vercessi's Hardware. Mr. Vercessi was trussed up with electrical wire and gagged with a kitchen sponge. He rolled this way and that on the floor of his store at Twenty-third. The two robbers took all they could carry. Every so often they emerged from the store bearing ball-peen hammers, drill bits, and torque wrenches, which they dumped in the back of a small red pickup, double-parked with the engine running. Mr. Vercessi had only $18 in his cash register. The robbers were so angry they could have killed him then and there. We can take some stuff, they said. We'll get something for the stuff.

It was two forty-five in the morning, and they had been at it since nine. Mr. Vercessi, about to close up for the night, had been alone in the store when the two men shouldered their way inside—one with a skeletal face white as chalk, the other speaking half in German, half in Japanese. The skeleton knocked Mr. Vercessi down with his fists. The bilingual one tied him up and shoved the sponge in his mouth. Then followed the enraged reaction to the cash, and the taking of the hardware. The skeleton considered clubbing Mr. Vercessi on the head with a length of pipe, but the bilingual one persuaded him not to.

Of course, I made all that up, but I had so little to go on, and the police, ever uncooperative, told me nothing as usual, treating me like a child. The following morning, I examined the scene of the crime while two cops in plainclothes asked questions of Mr. Vercessi. I was practiced in dealing with cases like that, so I scoured the sidewalk for clues and found a matchbook with handwriting on the inside cover, which I took home for further study under my magnifying glass. I did not mention it that night at dinner, when we sat as we always did—my parents, my brother, and I—saying not a word.

ONCE I WILLED a sequence of dreams in which I was an owl detective, both an owl and a detective. Nothing much happened in the dream. I remember hailing a taxi and telling the driver to "Follow that car" through the downtown streets, without ever catching "that car." As a largish owl, I had some difficulty stuffing my feathers into the taxi. But I was so happy with the experience when I woke up, that the following night, through sheer force of will, I had the same exact dream. And the night after that as well. And the night after that. Four nights in a row as an owl detective getting into a taxi and following a car into the impenetrable dark.

In *Speak, Memory,* Nabokov observes an aged swan, heavy and powerless, failing in its attempt to board a moored boat. He knows that the scene contains significance for him, but it is obscure—akin to moments in dreams when a finger is pressed against one's lips, and the finger points to an explanation that the dreamer has no time to receive before he awakens.

A MOMENT SUCH as now, in fact. That moment on a winter's day when the streetlights click on all at once, and you cannot help but smile. You might think that an awareness of the dark, just a moment before, would make you sad, half-sad at least. But the exuberant insistence of light, the brass of it, drives off gloom with a snap. Here I walk with the others of my city, heads high, backs straight. Let the cannon topple from the parapets. Let the owl fall into its feathers. Let the dreams begin and end. Big lights. Don't you love it? A penny for your thoughts.

For no reason at all, I think of Europe at this hour. And of the movie *Foreign Correspondent*—"Hang on to your lights, America. They're the only lights left in the world." The streetlights of London, Brussels, Prague, Budapest, lamps bowing from the neck like deacons. I don't know. They seem like ancient annotated texts, yet delve no deeper than the streetlights here, overlooking you and me. Somewhere in the city, your love lies sleeping in the curl of the night, and you proceed along Twenty-eighth Street gathering light like tulips, to bring to her bedside. She greets light in her dreams.

The street where lovers lost sight of each other was much

like this one. And the street where the villains with long knives stalked the waitress from the pub. Everyone walking from one pool of light toward another.

Clumsily I jump a patch of old snow stuck to a square in the sidewalk. Old snow, abandoned after the plows have cleared the streets. It hangs tough before it liquefies, clinging to the cornerstones, the bases of fountains, the knuckles of the statuary, in a last-man-standing gesture of self-assertion. Like the person who says "by the way" at the end of a conversation, introducing the subject he's wanted to speak of all along. The most important thing on his mind. Crusty, sooty detritus. A cold declension, but alive. Light falls on old snow. Are you with me, pal?

It is February 2011. And here I am again, walking the same streets I did as a boy. I have been teaching a class in memoir writing at Stony Brook University's Manhattan campus, on East Twenty-seventh Street. After class, I patrol the territory of my childhood. My home, my neighborhood of Gramercy Park, with its private, gated park that requires a key. Irving Place, named for Washington Irving and where he never lived. Madison Square, once the heart of upper-crust New York and where the Gilbert Hall of Science blazed, with its array of test tubes and bubbling amber liquids in great globes of glass. And the Lionel Train store and its smell of machine oil, and its nettings of tracks, whistles, and bridges. And Twenty-third Street, where the seedy novelty shops slouched in a row. And Twenty-fourth, the home of the Horse Market in the 1860s, and its modern remnants, two saddlery shops, Miller's and Kauffman's, with their gleaming saddles displayed on bright wood mounts. The dusky brownstones, aged gray by winter. The haberdasheries bearing headless manikins in ill-fitting shirts behind smudged glass. Met Life, the tallest building in the world till 1913. The Flatiron Building on Twenty-third, the tallest building before that, where the phrase "23 skidoo" originated, for the wind gusts caused by the triangular shape of the structure. Zoot-suiters would loiter at the point of the Flatiron to leer at women's skirts blown upward. Cops would shoo them away with "23 skidoo."

And Murray Hill, with its mixed air of elegance and menace. And the Village (no East Village in those days), boisterous, still Bohemian. And St. Marks Place, where my grandparents lived, and the old people—probably my age now—parked on folding chairs on the sidewalks in front of their tenements, and gossiping in Yiddish, Polish, German; the women with their thick legs exposed, brown stockings short of the knees. And Union Square, where I listened to a black man with hair like Uncle Ben of the rice box and a rich baritone give a speech about the modern enslavement of "the Negro." He was shirtless, wore a rope for a belt, and had tied himself up with chains. And Stuyvesant Park, cleaved in two by Second Avenue. And nearby Stuyvesant Town, home of Virginia Lee Jones—Ginny Jones, my best girl, with her shining brown hair, kind eyes, and noble bearing, my wife to be, mother of our children to be. All within walking distance in an area of New York, two and a half miles long and one mile wide, in which I first detected my life. Here I walk.

ON WALKING? "A walk is a way of entering the body, and also leaving it," said Edward Hirsch. That's very good. I walk within me and without. But how do you walk in the world? One foot in front of the other, declare the pragmatists. Yet in this life of ours, merely to become vertical requires two years, so any child can see that this walking business is not easy. Even when you get the hang of it, you still stumble and take headers. I read about a disabled boy named Walker who couldn't move a step, if you see what I mean. And, of course, the legless soldiers: How do they roll?

Sometimes I feel like the knotted cripples who drag themselves on crutches before congregations of thousands toward an altar festooned with tulips and a televangelist with a terrible pale face, who enunciates every letter of every word. He lays his hand on my head and beseeches heaven to save me. And then—would you believe it?—I feel the muscles tingle in my thighs, and very slowly I pull myself up, clinging to the shoulders of the preacher, and—praise Jesus!—I am standing, my crutches flung aside, and everyone is clapping and singing and weeping, until I take my first independent step, catch my foot on a nail, fall off the stage, and crack my pelvis in four places.

If you ask me, each of us has two souls, not one, and we take these two souls on our walks. One soul is for the senses, one for the intellect. So, our minds have a soul, which is our point of deepest thinking. And our hearts have a soul, which is our point of deepest feeling. They lead parallel lives, these two souls, never meeting yet connected, and side by side they move into infinity, like legs on a walk.

SAME OLD, SAME OLD. A man retraces the steps of his youth in order to determine where he has been and where he is. Your basic mystery story. Mixed motives, false leads, dead-end trails. Innocence is mistaken for guilt, guilt for innocence. Missing persons. Bodies everywhere. Only this particular mystery is endless, without crime, criminal, or justice. Words-worth uses a phrase in *The Prelude* that may apply to what I'm doing—"From hour to hour the illimitable walk / Still among Streets with cloud and sky above." He's speaking of walking in London, which, like New York, was and is as much an ideal as a reality, the place that is but also could be, should be. So, he refers to his wanderings as an "illimitable walk," meaning that if you commit yourself to wandering in the city, you cannot arrive anywhere, meaning also that you cannot *go* anywhere either. Like tracing a Möbius strip on which you can cover a good deal of ground, right side up and upside down, by going nowhere. But how *do* you walk in the world? Our lives runneth over with unsolved cases.

See, for starters, my parents' apartment at 36 Gramercy Park. From all outward appearances, it was gracious and open, like any big New York apartment built in the early 1900s. Eight large rooms with twelve-foot ceilings. French doors in the dining room. Gaslit fireplaces, with wisps of fake white ashes on the petrified logs. A narrow entrance hall leading to a grand foyer with a huge tubular chandelier painted unpolished gold. Wedgewood dinner plates propped up on little wooden stands. A midsize Steinway at the far end of the living room. Purple velvet on the window seats.

But there was also a secret panel in the dining room wall that concealed a small compartment, and a wall safe in my parents' bedroom that no one ever had opened, and a defunct dumbwaiter in the kitchen with a dark, empty shaft that ran the twelve-story height of the building. In my own room, a doorway had been covered and sealed with plywood and painted over. It led to the Homers' apartment on the opposite side of the floor. There were two apartments per floor. At one time, had the ninth floor of 36 Gramercy Park been one immense apartment, sixteen rooms? That seemed unlikely, because the two apartments were symmetrical. No one would plan an apartment with two identical foyers, two halls, two dining rooms and living rooms. So you tell me: Why the sealed door?

AND I TELL YOU: Gladly would I have forsaken the eight grand rooms in Gramercy Park for Sherlock Holmes's "lodgings" and "accommodations" at 221B Baker Street, consisting of "a couple of comfortable bedrooms and a single large airy sitting-room, cheerfully furnished and illuminated by two broad windows." Hell, I'd have been content with a one bedroom at 221A or 221C. I did not want to be one of Holmes's "Baker Street Irregulars," the gang of street kids he enlisted for help from time to time. I wanted to be Holmes, himself. The detective I concocted for myself was not exactly like him. What I imagined was a composite made up of Holmes's powers of observation, Hercule Poirot's powers of deduction, Sam Spade's straight talk, Miss Marple's stick-to-itiveness, and Philip Marlowe's courage and sense of honor—he who traveled the "mean streets," like mine, and was "neither tarnished nor afraid." The fact that, as far as I could tell, I lacked every single one of these qualities, and saw no prospect of ever achieving them, presented no discouragement.

The reason Holmes stood first among my shamus gods was, in part, that his were the first detective stories I ever read, understanding about one-third of each. But I easily grasped how well he lived, and how perfect was his setup on Baker

Street. If I was a bit unsure as to what "lodgings" and "accommodations" meant, to say nothing of a "sitting-room," the atmosphere of his life was clear. He was a "consulting detective." He sat at home puffing on his pipe and playing his violin until someone consulted him. And sure enough, someone always would. And that someone would be very important, such as Lord Saltire, the son of the duke of Holderness, whoever that was, and the king of Sardinia, wherever that was.

"Come in, Your Highness," I called from my chair, while the king remained outside the door of my lodgings and accommodations.

"But how did you know . . . ," he began as he entered my sitting-room.

"Your crown hit the door as you knocked, Your Excellency," I told him.

"Amazing, Mr. Holmes!" he said.

"Not to mention"—I smiled slightly—"the faintest odor of sardines."

NOT TO MENTION the faintest scent of brine, where I walk now. But what should one expect? This is Twenty-sixth Street, where Herman Melville lived at number 104, embittered for nearly thirty years. By the time he moved into his dreary one-bedroom flat, he had already written *White-Jacket, Pierre,* and *Moby-Dick.* The critics had flogged him. He had no money. He survived by working as a customs inspector, a job he described as "worse than driving geese to water." Eventually he finished *Billy Budd* five months before he died, in 1891. The book was found among his papers, and was not published till 1924. No evidence of his house today. The lot is occupied by an office building next to the 69th Regiment Armory, a blackened Moby-Dick of a building, where the International Exhibition of Modern Art was held in 1913, and where the neighborhood kids watched the New York Knicks in the early 1950s, before pro basketball got big.

Writers always have been drawn to the Gramercy Park area, which contained what Henry James, another resident, called "the incomparable tone of time." The park itself was a farm in the 1820s, bought by an entrepreneur, Samuel Ruggles, described as an advocate of open spaces, who spent $180,000 to drain the swamp on the property and create "Gramercy Square." This he deeded to the owners of forty-two parcels of land surrounding it. The park was enclosed by a fence in 1833, and a landscaper, with the demanding name of James Virtue, planted trees and shrubs, as well as privet hedges inside the fence to enforce the border. Apparently, Ruggles's definition of open spaces was limited to two acres (.08 hectares) of elaborately planned greenery and a gated Eden available only to those who lived directly around it and paid an annual fee for a key.

For myself, I could not stand the studied civility of the

place—the perfect rectangular park; the confident benches; the birdhouses, like restored Machu Picchu temples, one at each end; the gravel pathways running among four lawns cut in the shape of piano tops—exclusive, average, tame. That, above all, was what depressed me about Gramercy Park, more than its will for pointless order and enclosure and its smug prettiness—the feeling that the neighborhood might foster and contain creativity, but without the thrill of discovery, or self-discovery, or danger. Sea-level art. Gramercy Park seemed assured that it was better than anyone who lived there, with no evidence to support the assumption. Did Melville sense that as he walked these streets?

Yet the still, green neighborhood offered something for literary New York. Edith Wharton was born in a town house on the site of the Gramercy Park Hotel, now an apartment house on the north side of the park, in 1862. The sister poets, Phoebe and Alice Cary, moved here from Cincinnati in 1850, and established a literary salon that attracted such people as Horace Greeley, the editor of the *New York Tribune,* who advised young men to go west. Greeley had a three-story house at 35 East Nineteenth Street, and kept goats in his backyard. Stephen Crane moved in with three artists, in a run-down building on Twenty-third Street, where he found a fitting quotation from Emerson chalked on a wall: "Congratulate yourself if you have done something strange and extravagant and broken the monotony of a decorous age." The National

Arts Club, founded in 1898 on the south side of the park, included Mark Twain, W. H. Auden, and, more recently, Frank
McCourt among its members. E. B. White located *Stuart
Little* in Gramercy Park. Hard to know if Stuart counts as a
literary figure.

William Sydney Porter, O. Henry to his readers, lived
a bit better than most of the area writers, at 55 Irving Place,
because he had a steady job writing weekly stories for the *New
York World* at $100 a pop. He spent most of his time hanging
around Healy's Café across the street, and getting stinko with
fellow writers, artists, and musicians. Healy's Café became
Pete's Tavern, in which O. Henry was said to have written
"The Gift of the Magi." During Prohibition, Pete's posed as
a flower shop. Patrons walked past the cases of refrigerated
flowers on their way to the bar. Summers, when we were in
college, Ginny and I would sit here at the outdoor tables,
nurse beers, and speak of the life ahead of us. Tonight the
tables are cold and white with frost.

Oscar Wilde lived at Seventeenth Street and Irving
Place for a while. Minor literary figures, such as Carl Van
Vechten and Paul Rosenfield lived on Irving Place as well.
Local dinner parties were jazzed up by the likes of George
Gershwin, F. Scott Fitzgerald, Theodore Dreiser, Ethel Bar-
rymore, and Langston Hughes. They spilled gaily into what
Van Vechten had called "the splendid drunken twenties."
In 1927, Nathanael West took a position as night manager of

the fleabag Kenmore Hotel on Twenty-third, where he wrote *The Day of the Locust* and snuck other writers into the hotel. Dashiell Hammett registered under the name Mr. T. Victoria Blueberry. West gave him the swankiest suite in the joint, where Hammett wrote *The Maltese Falcon*—telling of wicked women, murderers, and treasure three blocks from where Herman Melville, PI, alone and unnoticed, had tracked evildoers down the vast gray streets of the sea.

To this precious place, Dr. Milton B. Rosenblatt brought his bride, Mollie Ruth Spruch, in 1939, one year before I was born. Suspicious characters, both. Even their names were aliases. My mother was born Marta, but when she entered grade school, the authorities told my German grandparents that Marta was not an American name, as compared to, say, Mollie. No one seemed to know where my father came from. Whenever I asked, the answer was different each time. Sometimes Poland, sometimes Russia, occasionally Lithuania. As for *his* alias, the B. stood for Barrington, which he picked up on a drive through Great Barrington, Massachusetts. He thought the name gave him WASPy class, which he both sought and derided. He rises from his own ashes, my fastidious father, and dusts himself off.

He wore three-piece suits. He wore hats from Cavanaugh's—gray felt hats in the winters and straw skim-

mers in the summers. He wore neckties indoors, and smoking jackets, sitting alone in the silent home he made. I have
a photograph of him when he was two or three, wearing a
girl's dress as all infants did in those days. He looked old even
then, with his grim, displeased expression and his Edward
G. Robinson jowls. As a child, I was expected to be old, too.
"Roger," he said one day, "that's no way for a twelve-year-old
boy to behave." "Dad," I said, "I'm eight."

So angry was he with life, his fury often came out funny.
All my childhood, I was assailed by his rules for successful
living, such as "Never trust a Hungarian." At the age of three,
it was hard to know how to apply such advice. In my teens, he
told me, "Never go out with anyone from Brooklyn," which
expanded to include the Bronx, Queens, and New Jersey as
well. Reared on Manhattan's Lower East Side, he hated that
fact, too. He spent his remaining years trying to get away
from the poverty associated with the Lower East Side, and to
shake off Judaism as if it were a local curse. He wanted to be
up and out. Up from DeWitt Clinton High School. Up from
City College, where he was a boxer. When he became a doctor, he and my mother moved up in the world to Gramercy
Park, where he had his first office. Later, he moved his office
farther uptown, to 1040 Fifth Avenue at Eighty-fifth Street.
When Jackie Kennedy moved into the building in 1964, he
complained about the Secret Service men. He hated them.
He hated her, with whom, of course, he never spoke. He was

made chief of medicine at Doctors Hospital, the ritziest if not the most efficient hospital in the city. Ever combative, he told me he won the position "over all the Harvards and Yales."

In the 1960s, when I was in my twenties, he became a neocon Republican like many FDR Democrats, and was sneeringly contemptuous of every liberalizing event I celebrated. Often we would argue late into the night, and although I was in the right in our arguments, he always managed to gain the upper hand. One evening, we were seated next to each other in identical red upholstered chairs, watching the seven o'clock news, when Alabama's governor George Wallace came on. This was in 1968, before Wallace had been shot, saw the light, and was crowned a "national treasure." In those days he was purely a fearmonger with sweet talk. When he addressed the nation, as he did for a full three minutes that evening, you knew you were getting hate and death, unsullied by platform politics. My father, not taking his eyes from the TV screen, thought for a moment, giving himself just the right pause. Finally he said, "You know, in a decent country a jackass like that would not be given ten seconds on television. But now, thanks to you liberals, he can talk his brains out."

WHOA! SPEAKING OF TALKING: Here's a guy, underdressed for the weather in jeans, a T-shirt, and a blazer, quickstepping up Thirtieth and braying into his cell in behalf of a business deal he hopes to pull off. I can't make out the particulars. He yammers on into a small crowd ahead of me, gaining speed, and explaining about how "It's a *lock,* Phil" and "Let's just *do* it!" It is evident that Phil is not ready to just do it, if he ever will be, and sensing this, our public speaker grows louder and more dramatic in his self-promotion. A self-revving engine. The crowd expects that he'll take off. And just as this thought occurs, why *yes*, his left foot rises on the air and then his right, and all at once he is lifting into the cold dark, two or three inches off the ground, speaking ever more urgently. "You don't see this *happening*, Phil? Of *course* you do! Of *course* you do!"

At first, finding him merely pathetic, I listen to his pitch with a disinterested malice, waiting for his voice to sink in despair as he grows aware of his inevitable failure. Phil says no, emphatically. My man droops his head, held so high until that moment. But now, as he approaches Thirty-second, I find myself quietly cheering his lusty desperation, as if he were speaking for all mankind knocking its head against a brick wall. And you can feel others on the street pulling for him, too, though not a syllable of encouragement is uttered. In his relentless effort to win Phil over, he has become the leader of our pack of strangers, our head bird. We are swept along in his tail wind. "Come *on,* Phil. You *know* it's going to happen. It's *gotta* happen!"—the last words we hear from him as he goose-steps toward the moon.

IF YOU DON'T want to be around people who talk their
brains out, why live in New York? Talking freely is the city's
thing—you can feel it—what the city does, and has done from
the start, when the Dutch carried the prizes of tolerance and
openness from Holland across the Atlantic and planted those
bright, fat tulips here. Free thought became free markets. The
Dutch republic of the 1600s boasted the most gloriously di-
verse culture in Europe. Bertrand Russell called seventeenth-
century Holland the birthplace of "freedom of speculation."
I cannot claim that as a boy I was aware of any of this history,
but even a nine-year-old could feel the city's extravagant freedom in the air—every block, every home inviting you to speak
your mind. On my detective's walks, though I hardly knew it,
I strutted as a young colonial, escaping the tyranny of a silent
house.

Who, after all, is more suited to the liberal life than the
detective, who, by dint of his very profession, defies restric-
tions of government, of the police, and of conventional, pre-
dictable thinking? If in some ways detectives are also arch
conservatives, in that they tame the behavior of their clients,
indeed tame society itself, and make it orderly, still, they
function according to their own rules of honor and justice arrived at independently. The private enterprise of the private
op. Every detective story depends on their freedom of speculation without which no mystery can be solved.

As I wandered the city on my cases, I did not think that

I existed anywhere other than where I happened to be at the time—in Madison Square Park or the Village or Murray Hill or St. Marks Place. Yet I could not help but sense that I was also treading a path that had been laid out before me centuries earlier by those who believed the human mind was built to confront mysteries. The detective story is that of free speculation at work. And the Dutch wrote it for the world long before Holmes pursued Moriarty, or I, the bad guys of my own manufacture.

You'd think it would have been Edgar Allan Poe who coined the word *detective,* because Poe wrote the first detective stories, that is, stories with the now-familiar components of the know-it-all sleuth, the invaluable stooge or sidekick, the bumbling police, and so forth. But though Poe created "Murders in the Rue Morgue," "The Purloined Letter," and "The Gold Bug," along with C. Auguste Dupin, the little genius who solved his crimes, the term for Dupin was not *detective.* Poe might have used that term had he written his mysteries after 1843. That was when Sir James Graham, the British home secretary, seeking to give the ablest officers in the London police force a special designation, formed a unit called "the detectives." Even if Poe had known the word, he would not have pinned it on Dupin without prefixing the word *private,* because, like all great independent or "consulting" detectives, Dupin never would have been associated with the police. A detective worth his salt has no use for institutions—not only because he's smarter than the institutions, but also because he cannot survive in a group.

Take Dupin himself, who in fact was not an amateur sleuth or committed to crime fighting in any way. He was more like an unemployed philosopher, equipped with the reasoning intelligence Poe called "ratiocination," and driven by a near-manic curiosity. A collector of rare books, he had retreated from Parisian society until he chanced to meet the person who turned out to be the narrator of "Murders in the Rue Morgue." Thence, Dupin's legacy.

When I first took up the trade as a boy, I wondered about the word *detective,* as *detector* might have seemed more fitting. You wouldn't say "lie detective." The suffix *-ive* suggests something or someone performing a specific action, or a condition, such as in *defective* or *directive* or *corrective.* But what makes the word right, I think, is that *detective* seems more detached than *detector,* which intimates a more personal passion. A true detective had better not care too much about the cases he's involved in, lest he lose the objectivity that gives him his powers. Hard-boiled private eyes often come perilously close to falling for one dame or another, and sometimes there is a hint of a great love in the past. Holmes's heart held Irene Adler of "A Scandal in Bohemia," referred to afterward, with a pang, as "the woman." Yet, to do his work effectively and dispassionately, the detective must remain the detective. He walks at an even pace. He measures his steps with a cold eye.

Now that I think of it, that quality of self-control might explain why Poe wrote detective stories in the first place. A wild man in everything else he did, he turned his pen to stories of orderly expectations and rational deductions. Could it be that he saw the world as frenzied and manic, and by creating the detective story, he felt he could contain that chaos within the seemingly immutable laws of reason? Or maybe he invented the detective story as a way of holding madness at arm's length, to avoid going crazy himself. There is justice in a detective story, and none in madness. And while there is danger in a detective story, it eventually is put to rest, which distinguishes a detective story from life, where the mysteries are illimitable.

HERE'S WHAT I mean: Twenty-ninth Street between Madison and Park Avenue South. Something fishy about this block. That so-called health club, Exhale—a "mind-bodyspa." I'll bet. And the storefront notice that an artist has posted as an ad for his photographs, taken in New Mexico, describing them as "a metaphor for the timeless interior landscape of the mind." This is code, don't you think? And what monkey business goes on at the low, wide office building that purports to contain the Community Prep High School "for learners and leaders"? And what should we make of this? Stampworx. The *x*. And this: Technetron Electronics. What's cooking here, I'd like to know. The graffiti on a couple of walls: SIN and ETAH (*hate* backward). Somebody's picking up a message, no? And the three-story red town house with the soldered metal door. Yet the windows have air conditioners. Who lives there?

While we're at it, in what country is this block? On the southeast corner, an eight-story, glacierlike apartment house with tiers of Plexiglas balconies, called the Gansevoort (The Netherlands). And Gansevoort happened to be Melville's mother's maiden name, as well as that of his brother. What should we make of that? Next door, Winston's "La Maison de Champagne" (France). Across the street, a parking garage (Mexico), beside a two-story house with a roll-down metal door and a red fire escape out front leading up to a square iron balcony like Juliet's (let's say England). And next to that, another town house with a sign NEW AGE INNER VISION, and a picture of gypsies (let's say Romania, or Hungary), which sits beside the Lalabla restaurant (Ethiopia), which sits across the street from La Campanile (Italy). And down the block, the Lola Hotel (who knows?) next door to the Habib American Bank (Egypt?), across from a grand old office building called The Emmet (Ireland). In the middle of the block, on the north side of the street, stands the Permanent Mission of Moldova to the United Nations (Moldova). Moldova, my foot. Something's up here, I swear. I smell a rat.

HERE'S LOOKING at you, city of going going going. City of gorgeous surprises and oh-Jesus! coincidences, such as bumping into people you know or haven't seen for years, in the place where millions walk. Or bumping into Elizabeth Bishop's "Letter to N.Y." as you are poring over the copyedited manuscript of a memoir—where she writes of "taking cabs in the middle of the night . . . and the meter glares like a moral owl."

DID YOU KNOW that Detective Poe was involved in a real murder case, in the 1840s? A man named John Anderson had a tobacco shop near Duane Street on lower Broadway. In his employ was a twenty-year-old woman named Mary Cecilia Rogers, whose good looks were so well known she was celebrated in the city. A writer for the *New York Herald* described her "heaven-like smile and her star-like eyes," and she was dubbed the "Beautiful Cigar Girl." However heavenly Mary appeared, her activities were more terrestrial, involving several men of low reputation, as they put it in those days.

On July 28, 1841, Mary's body was found floating in the Hudson. She had been the victim of either a brutal gang beating, as initially thought by the police, or of a botched abortion, or both. One suspect was Daniel Payne, a cork cutter and a drunk, who lived at the boardinghouse run by Mary and her mother. Payne took poison shortly after Mary's death, but he'd had an alibi for the night she died.

Enter Poe, who, along with Washington Irving and James Fenimore Cooper, frequented Anderson's cigar emporium and was said to be smitten with the Beautiful Cigar Girl. He would question Anderson about her incessantly. A year or so after her death, Poe published "The Mystery of Marie Rogêt"—Mary Rogers—in which Dupin proved that the girl was murdered by a young naval officer who earlier had tried to elope with her. In the story, he had dragged her body to the river after the botched abortion. Poe's version became the accepted solution to the murder, but it was just a story. No one ever solved the case. Some thought Poe had killed her himself. I may be making this up.

ALL RIGHT, I did it. I killed her. But it was an accident. Sort of. Sort of an accident. I didn't mean to do it, but I did. That is, I did mean to do it, but I didn't. If you want to arrest someone, why don't you nab that naval officer who knocked her up? And I didn't even care about that. I mean, I would have liked to be the first, but with Mary, that would have taken an awfully early arrival. I didn't want her to have the abortion either. I was perfectly willing to live with her and the baby, in a little place I have on Third Street, or another in the Bronx. Anywhere. We could have made a life together. I would have given up booze.

But when I said all that to her, pleaded with her that night down by the river, where I had pursued her . . . when I said all that—and I was sober as a judge—she laughed. She said, Why would I marry a skin-and-bones doped-up drunk who gets his rocks off by writing about life instead of living it? And when I told her that art was more important than life, she laughed harder, because she could see in my maddened eyes that I didn't mean a word of it, that I would have tossed away all the poems, all the stories, for the love, the real love, of a woman. She saw that—the tobacco girl. She understood intuitively that I'd become a writer because no one would love me. And that insight of hers was at once so saddening and enraging to me that I put my hands on her throat, her white, white throat. And at that point she spun away and freed herself from my grasp and stood there, and danced a taunting little jig. But as she did, she slipped on a wet rock and cracked her head half open. What was I to do? I pushed her body in the water, and went home.

All I wanted was her heart. Now I hear it beating in the walls of my room. But you know that.

ONCE IN A rare while my boy detective would actually solve a mystery, insofar as mysteries can be solved, as in the case of the bent old woman—black coat, black dress—who used to walk around Gramercy Park hurriedly, as if she were chasing something. She muttered to herself, occasionally looking up to see the kids of the neighborhood staring at her, and mocking her. "There's the witch," we said. "Witch!" And she would shake her tiny fist at us and walk on, never slowing, around and around the park.

One Saturday afternoon when I was ten and alone, I watched from a distance as she made her rounds. Eventually she veered off and headed toward Twenty-third Street, then up to Twenty-sixth and Park (no Park Avenue South in those days either) to the Horn & Hardart Cafeteria. I followed. She looked to the left and to the right and entered, moving in spurts to the wall of food behind the little glass doors. She dipped her hand into her black purse, extracted several coins, and, with great care, pushed them into one of the slots, opening the little glass door tentatively, as if she were about to be surprised by what lay behind it. She removed a thick wedge of cheesecake on a heavy cream-color plate, and studied it. Then she looked to the right and left again, and, determining that it was safe, moved to a corner table, away from others in the cafeteria, and slowly ate. After that, I tried to dissuade the other kids from calling her the witch—after seeing her and the wedge of cheesecake on the heavy cream-color plate before her, at a table in the Horn & Hardart Cafeteria.

Do dead spirits walk among us? What's your opinion, pal? From time to time I catch them moving on the streets, dodging cars, and potholes, though for the life of me I can't see why. What on earth do ghosts have to fear? You wonder if people live with one another or with these spirits. A topic of my memoir class. Everyone dwells in one past or another, and to a greater or lesser extent, is ruled by it. The coarse sleeve of her long black coat. It touches my arm. I shiver. Ghosts address a man on a walk.

Were I to believe in reincarnation, what would it be like for reborn me to walk these streets again? Would there come to the brand-new mind and body—the Iraqi girl's, the wheaten terrier's—a breeze of recollection of my former life, my life as it is now? Would it be a simple flash of déjà vu? Or something more vague, like a tremor of unease, attributed to no objective experience, born only of itself? From time to time, I feel that chill today, so perhaps it is a sign that we live once and again. It better suits me to see such moments as parts of dreams. They may well be dreams.

In my sleep, my father appears two or three times a year, never confronting me directly. I simply watch him or overhear him as he declaims on one topic or another. Then I wake into dreams, and he is clearer to me. If I concentrate, I probably could see all the ghosts of my life, here at the corner of Thirty-first and Madison, bundled in their winter coats, huddled in a scrum, all of us waiting for the light to change.

FOR THAT MATTER, I may be a ghost of my own life. Since we never leave our childhood, I see myself as a boy on these streets I walk now as a man. I am the spitting image of myself. How like myself I am. This is why I do not believe in time. How could I if I feel the presence of the boy as completely as I do the man, in many ways more completely since the boy is more completely realized. He who existed in me over half a century ago walks with me today.

But it makes sense, doesn't it? We live through future generations, so why shouldn't past generations live through us? It may be as much of immortality as we can expect, or bear. On this walk, whenever I pass a restaurant with high marble walls and pressed tin ceilings, I know the building was a bank a hundred years ago. I see the restaurant, I see the bank. Possibly it was a trading house a hundred years before that, dealing in horses or slaves. Might have been a cathouse before it was a trading house. Don't think of it as history. Rather, see the whores, the horses and slaves, the potbellied bankers and the careful eaters as one—all of life packed into a crowded present, each iteration reachable by a mere flick of the imagination. The point is, though time was invented to keep things from happening all at once, things do happen all at once, and all the clocks in the world, including the one at Greenwich, England, can't do a thing about it. Boy detective, man detective, writer, god-knows-what. Questions then, unanswered now.

So you can ask me till you are blue in the face, but I have no explanation as to why I sat at the kitchen window at the back of the vast apartment, day after day, that looked out over the courtyard nine stories below, and beyond, past the blackened wooden water tanks on the rooftops of other buildings to the east, and toward the river. There I would remain for hours at a stretch, parked at the windowsill that was a slab of veined marble, white, gray, and darker gray, studious, purposeful, using a butter knife to chisel away at a crack in the marble until the underneath was exposed like the bones of birds. I gouged a crevice, a dark valley in the shape of a delta that deepened and widened with every day's effort. It may have appeared that I was digging for something buried in the slab. A clue? A finger-print? Something. For the life of me, I cannot remember what.

JUST ANOTHER CASE. Open and shut or, more like it, shut and open. Everything is a case. A while ago I was chatting up this meter maid, name of Marisol (her badge), when a guy slammed his Accord into a Civic right before our eyes. Accord, my ass! I nearly said to Marisol. But I held my tongue lest she conclude that I was some candy-ass intellectual, which I sometimes am, or, almost as bad, a cop. It's easy to mistake us private eyes for cops. So I said, "Shit! Did you see that!" And she said, "Twice a day at least," while smiling a smile at once coquettish and indicative of "Look, mister, I need to get back to work." And I didn't intend to keep her, but "I wanted to ask you," I said, "what alternate-side-of-the-street parking means, since I hear that phrase on the traffic reports every morning. What exactly constitutes the alternate side?" And the look she gave me, full of contempt and pity, should have been enough to tell me that if you really want to understand the city, or your life for that matter, you need to solve your own mysteries.

No MYSTERY TO the Empire State, except that tall as it is, the building never surprises you. Perhaps that's because it is old and familiar, the city's favorite uncle, who just plants himself in the middle of the house. Standing on Thirty-fourth Street, I look up to it as ever. Its feeling of calm comfort is what appealed to King Kong, I am sure of it. Not the height, though he might have experienced a wave of fellow feeling with the tallest thing around for miles. He might have thought, This building knows how difficult, how demanding, how embarrassing it is to be the gorilla in the room. In that case, it could be assumed that King Kong did not so much scale the Empire State as embrace it. So that might have been his reason.

But I think it was something else. I mean, here was this big ape and here was the big uncle of New York City, the old man who implied merely by being: You are safe with me, King Kong. And even if it turns out that you aren't safe, even if you clamber to the top of me, your massive hairy hand enclosing Faye Wray, with one last chance at love within your grasp, and a swarm of biplanes swoop down out of nowhere and *ack-ack* at you, and you holding on to my rooftop pike where the blimps tied up, and you begin to lose your grip—even then, it will be all right. You have lived long enough, King Kong. A good life. A big life. The biggest. If you must fall, fall from me.

UNREAL NEW YORK. E. B. White's famous essay "Here Is New York," which is neither half good nor half bad, keeps thumping away at the loneliness of the city and attaches loneliness to privacy. I, born and reared here, have never thought of the city in terms of loneliness and privacy. Perhaps those who hail from outside New York, like White, find things opposed to the life they led wherever they came from. Communities do not exist in the same ways in New York as they do in small towns or smaller cities, where their demands for conformity are more blatant and melodramatic. Transplanted to the big city, the out-of-towner thinks he's discovered loneliness and privacy by way of contrast.

Not I. Loneliness and privacy are real, whereas to me it is the unreality of New York that thrills the citizen soul. Wake up, dress, walk out your door, and there you are, my owl, in an area such as the one I wander in now, bathed in an unreal light. The trouble with those who associate New York with a certain condition or goal is that they are in search of conditions or goals. Real New Yorkers do not want anything of the city. Oh, White loved New York, no doubt about that. But he loved it like a swain who has noted and studied everything about the object of his affection, and then found pleasant words to make cohesive sense of the experience. New Yorkers abjure cohesiveness. We think in images, like detectives. We reason with our senses.

Want to know the city? A silver-haired gamine stands at the top of the steps of a brownstone apartment house, on the south side of Eighteenth, between Second and Third. She wears black sweatpants and a sailor's pea jacket a couple of sizes too big. I have been watching her for five minutes, and she hasn't moved an inch. Just stands there in the black arch of the doorway to the brownstone, craning her neck to the left, toward Third, as if she were on a railroad station platform in rural Alabama, or Arizona, or Russia, waiting for the arrival of a train. The night wind could lift her like a sheet of paper and float her on the cold air over the street, over everything. But she stands her ground. Nothing can shake her or divert her from her purpose—the woman at the top of the steps, peering to her left, and waiting for a train. *Here* is New York.

WHO OWNS THIS city, anyway? To go by the self-possessed Fifth Avenue apartment houses and the office buildings on Third, with their shit-eating grins, the answer is easy. Big people own this city. But since there are a lot more little people strolling around in New York, you could say that the city belongs to the vast unnoticed. Yet they are noticed here. Everyone is noticed in New York. You could focus the question on Dominicans. Surely they own the city. Or the Chinese. Or Puerto Ricans, Hassids, Mexicans, Koreans, Muslims. The African Americans definitely own New York. You can tell by the way they walk, the muted swagger. You can tell by the way everybody walks. Every citizen is a Dutch patroon inspecting his property. How about young versus old? Both are well represented on every block of my territory, where a cigar store from the 1940s nudges up against a granite mansion put up last month. Who, then?

You there! (See that rake standing like Jimmy Walker, his top hat tilted down on his forehead, supported by his silver walking stick? See his spats?) You! Jimmy Walker. *Walker*. You own this city, don't you, you sly devil? I thought so.

I PUT IT to my memoir students: In what do you believe if not in dreams? The pluperfection of experience? The so-called reality of your life? Surely, you're not saying that you believe in things you can see, touch, hear—things that happen in the world. The kiss? The firing squad? Who could possibly believe in them? Ask yourself if they ever really happened—the embrace, the knife, the tulip. Take an autobiographical inventory of all the disconnected moments, and they will seem like what? A dream. But dreams themselves, which bind the moments together in a night, and blur the tenses—dreams are real. And one reason to use them in your memoir—daydreams, night dreams—is that it allows others, your readers, to enjoy their own dreams without shame.

So what is the difference, students, between memory and dreams? Are they not the same, each the other? Or will you tell me that memories are accurate and dreams are mere impressions? Of course, you will not. You have never had an accurate memory in your life, whereas your dreams are always on the money. Which is why you wake up in a sweat. Which is why Nabokov held sleep in such contempt. He claimed to hate sleep as an evasion of reality, but I think he hated the reality of dreams. He, too, did not believe in time. How does one dismiss time and dreams, both, since dreams, too, do not believe in time? Such a strange detective.

GINNY HAD A dream in which she learned (she did not say how) that what she was dreaming constituted the real world, and that the world into which she would awaken constituted a dream. Furthermore, it came to her (she did not say how) that this reversal of states of being made sense to her, since she understood so little of the waking life, she might as well be dreaming. To be sure, one does not find that much understanding in a dream, either, though there usually is a moment of calm or distance when one acknowledges that one is, in fact, dreaming. That, I suppose, is a form of understanding. The problem (is there a problem?) . . . the problem may lie in the criteria for understanding in the first place. If reality is defined by our understanding of experience, of anything at all, well, that's one thing. But if reality is simply a prolonged state of confusion, why not go for dreams, where mysteries are taken for granted?

And just as I am trying to work all this out—about dreams and reality, I mean—a scrawny woman in a flower-print dress and a hat with a blue ostrich feather accosts me, gets right up in my face, and asks if I was the one who shot Abe Lincoln. And I say, "Me? Shoot Abe Lincoln? Why, you jackass, Abe Lincoln was done in a hundred and fifty years ago. Do I look a hundred and fifty years old to you?" Make that one hundred and seventy-five years ago, since I would have had to be at least twenty-five when I shot the president. "So you *did* shoot him," she said, her voice crackling like cellophane, and trembling with such loathing it filled the street with smoke and darkness. And I tell you: I was more afraid of that look of hers, and her rattling bones, than I ever was the night I leapt from the Ford's Theatre balcony and broke my leg, after plugging Honest Abe in the ticker.

Is HE A memory or a dream—southern, courtly Carroll, the doorman at 36 Gramercy, who wore his gray uniform with the epaulets like a soldier, like Emil Jannings in *The Door-man,* only Carroll was gentle and proud to be what he was. That was when people were proud to be what they were. Much of my little life was spent with Carroll greeting my mother and me and the other residents with such official politeness. He stood tall like a column of mercury in front of two gray stone knights on pedestals, who guarded the building with him. Above him was a long dark green awning. So dramatically classy was Carroll that a director put him in a movie for which they were using number 36—*East Side, West Side*—with James Mason, as the philandering husband of Barbara Stanwyck, on whom he cheats with Ava Gardner. My building was in the opening scene, as Mason and Stanwyck arrived in a yellow taxi. The movie people had cordoned off the entrance. I stood in a crowd beside my mother. Turner Classic Movies showed *East Side, West Side* some years ago. I watched it to see Carroll open a taxi door as no one could ever open a taxi door, and shut it as no one could ever shut it.

BEHOLD THE upright people.

    Behold their dogs.

    Make way for princes, to say nothing of kings.

    Say nothing of kings.

    Prosperous folks to the left.

Phosphorous folks to the right. Stay in line, please.

"Hello, Charlie! Howzitgoin?"

Behold the military heroes, women as well as men.

And the citizens of Gramercy Park in their frightful dignity, and the trees with their shorn boughs shaking. Behold them.

I love a parade.

MORTON STAMPS. WHAT the painted sign read in the barely lit hallway. What Mr. Morton called his one-room shop on Twenty-third between Park and Madison. Tonight I stand looking up at the whitewashed window no longer his, which bears an incomprehensible sign: WWW.UNDISPUTEDCORP. And beneath that: FOR RENT. Morton Stamps. The shop was like a hideout, located one long flight up a metal staircase. Mr. Morton hardly acknowledged me when I entered, which was at least twice a week when I was eleven and twelve. He never addressed me by name, just stood behind the glass-and-wood cabinets in which the stamps were displayed. Heavy and bald, his face bearing no character, like linoleum. I took to him the way children take to people who do not like children. He regarded me only as a paying customer—the meager dollar or two I could spend on the cheapest stamps. I don't know why I collected stamps. I am not a collector by nature. I think I simply enjoyed looking at them. The colorful ones from Ivory Coast and Togo. And the German stamps, with the profiles of Hitler.

He was German, Morton; his accent was German. A war criminal perhaps—Morton stamps on Jews—or a Jewish refugee himself. I had my eye on him. I took notes. Nazi or Jew, he was secretive and dour enough for either, like the man who outlived the concentration camps in *The Pawnbroker* and who slammed his hand on the pike that held store receipts, to see if he had any feeling left. Never did I encounter another customer in Morton Stamps. I would sidle silently from display case to display case, peering in for half an hour or more. Morton would watch me through eyeglasses with thick brown rims. Occasionally he would produce what he thought was an interesting stamp within my price range. Usually I went away with prepackaged bags of the cheapest stamps, hoping that the one with the upside-down biplane, the most valuable stamp in the world, had slipped in by mistake.

At the Jerusalem Book Fair in 1985, Milan Kundera surveyed the gorgeous auditorium of gleaming wood, addressed the attendees, and said he was looking at all the culture of Europe. I sat with other writers in the audience. Several people wept. What time is it in Israel? What time is it here? Do you have the time? What time was it when my Berliner cousins, whose names I will never know, were hauled off to Birkenau and tossed into ovens, while I played capture the flag in Gramercy Park? Was it the same time? By your watch, I mean.

NOT THAT ANY of this could explain Ira Fink, one of the neighborhood kids who used to play with us in the park and blurt out, "I'm Hitler!," after which we all would pummel him. No one was quite sure why Ira, otherwise a nice, quiet kid, would ask for it by claiming to be Hitler, unless it was an attention-getting device, which certainly worked. The matter was made more confusing whenever we played hide-and-seek, and Ira would yell, "I'm hit" instead of "it." Did he have a speech impediment that caused him to mispronounce *h*'s? If so, when he was announcing that he was the Führer, was he really saying, "I'm Itler," which made even less sense? In any case, Ira reminded us kids that a war was going on. He, and the radio news reports, and the air raid drills—my father with his warden's armband, the neighborhood pitch-dark.

Something you learn in the detective game: Everything deadly turns funny eventually. One evening Liz Smith was doing her TV gossip column. She deadpanned: "We've just learned that Claus von Bülow was a ring bearer in Hermann Göring's wedding. I know it's boring," she said, "but we get so few social notes from the Third Reich these days."

THE LONELINESS OF the private eye is not the same as God's. One may only guess whether or not God is lonely in his uniqueness. He may be so removed from the concept that he has no idea (does God have ideas?) what loneliness means, or what companionship means, for that matter, or the love or contempt of others. But the private eye, whose distinction of privacy applies equally to his clients and his nature, he does know loneliness. Earlier in his life, he has been with others—a wife, friends, the police force itself—and, for one reason or another, he now finds himself alone. And he discovers that he prefers to be alone, for only in aloneness can he pursue and judge purely. He is not godlike in this, after all. He is the god who interferes.

Read Sam Spade's speech at the end of *The Maltese Falcon,* when he tells Brigid O'Shaughnessy that she is "going over" for shooting Miles Archer, Sam's partner. Brigid cannot believe that Sam means it. She loves him and he loves her, she says. Be that as it may, Sam tells her, the practical truth is that if he protects her she will have something to hold over him for the rest of their lives, and one day, if she fears he might betray her, she might shoot him, too. But that is not the main reason for turning her in. When a man's partner is killed, he says, he has to do something about it. There's a code about such things. So over goes Brigid O'Shaughnessy.

And here, you see, is where Sam's loneliness comes in. Had he not been a solitary man making that decision, who knows what he would have done with his loving, lovely murderess? He might have consulted an outsider, who might have advised him to choose love over honor. It's been done. He might have paid attention to an outside world that often does value love over honor. He might have wanted to fit into a larger society where questions of love and honor are easily and intentionally confused. But Sam Spade was all by himself, which is the only place for the straight shooter.

Signs of progress, I suppose—all these shiny new apartment buildings in the East Twenties and Thirties. The entrances look like Egyptian tombs, each building rising like a rocket thirty stories and more, and flipping the sky the bird. They stand in place of the vacant lots we played in as kids, and of the vacant tenements with the plywood eyes. And nostalgie de la boue is silly, though I cannot help but wonder where all the poor people went during this spectacular urban redevelopment. The rich stay rich, and the homeless constitute a sect of their own. But the poor, the simple poor, used to have a place around here as well. Even Gramercy Park had its share, in the days of genteel poverty and elbow patches and rehemmed dresses. Everything we see in the world stirs something in us. Don't you think so, pal? I am moved by the shiny new buildings as I once was moved by the pitch of a tar roof. I am moved by the young women successes caressing their iPhones, as I was moved by their grandmothers leaning out the windows, with their deflated breasts on the rotted sills, and shrieking for their dogs to come home. The trees remain as they were, I think. Many of the same trees. I am moved by them as well, and by their branches, which now tilt downward.

A pigeon commands my attention. Yet I am not zeroing in on it, because that would require conscious exclusivity. A detective learns how to look at things. I wish to see the pigeon, so I do. But there is another kind of attentiveness, a shamus attentiveness that simultaneously takes in the pigeon and all that surrounds the pigeon. Pigeon history and anthropology. The genealogies of pigeons worldwide. I apply dual focus, of far and near objects. I see the pigeon, and I also see where he is going and where he has been. To achieve this sort of sight, I empty my mind and grow accustomed to the dark.

Later, if the moon is shrouded, you may be able to see the National Arts Club, its sandstone blocks glowing dimly like old leather. Gothic. Mournful. The stone-guarded windows, the facades of mausoleums.

Or, turn to the little red brick town houses on the west side of Gramercy Park, standing like Napoleonic soldiers, like lifeguards with swimmers' bodies, short and muscular, tidy little houses, where some of my friends lived. The father of one was a ham operator. He had an elaborate radio setup and he was happy to show us kids how it worked—a little too happy, if you'd asked me. First staticky, then clear, the radio was like the ones I'd seen in spy movies. The son did not seem interested in his father, the spy. But it was my business to take note of such people. I was also curious about the boy who lived next door to him. Big kid, a galoot, he had a nervous tic of holding his face in his hands and molding his flesh, the way one kneads dough. Something going on there? On this cold night, the little red brick town houses are neat as pins, with their wrought-iron New Orleans fences and their empty window boxes. Go and admire them. You are only human.

THE PLACES WE leave go on being themselves after we leave them. Imagine that. They do not drown in creeks of tears at our departure. They do not apologize for being so dull and cruel, or whatever the reasons we gave for our leaving them. They do not even notice that we left. Knowing this does not affect our decision, of course. We were bound to be exiles, and we have stuck to our guns. Good riddance, we say. The deserted places say nothing. The world does not change according to the way we see it.

The people we leave go on being themselves after we leave them. Imagine that. And all the influence we exerted upon them, all the delicate maneuvers we pulled off, go away in a trice. Cavafy tells us that the Poseidonians, after centuries of mingling with the corrupting Tyrrhenians and Romans, forgot the Greek language, which they had spoken for centuries before. Only an annual festival recalled the Greek presence, which once had been ubiquitous and deep. Do the people we leave hold a residual festival for us? I doubt it. They merely become the barbarians we always suspected they were before we left. Why do we leave anything? Yet we leave everything.

EXCEPT AFGHANISTAN, of course. One never leaves Afghanistan. In *Moby-Dick,* old Melville listed his headlines—GRAND CONTESTED ELECTION FOR THE PRESIDENCY OF THE UNITED STATES, WHALING VOYAGE BY ONE ISHMAEL, and BLOODY BATTLE IN AFGHANISTAN. He chose Afghanistan because it has always seemed the most faraway place on earth, perhaps at times to the Afghans themselves. In 1851, when *Moby-Dick* was published, presidential elections must have seemed equally remote to the average citizen; thus by arranging his items on the bill, Melville was also posing a question: What could the story of one solitary citizen possibly have to do with the big and violent doings of the world? The connections between Ishmael's Afghans and presidents are rarely seen until too late, least of all by the Ishmaels who go about their solitary businesses deliberately to avoid the big and violent doings.

Ishmael minimized the significance of his adventure, yet that turned out to offer as grand a contest, as bloody a battle as any. It was the essential journey—the pursuit of the nemesis. The Moriarty. It was not Ishmael's nemesis being pursued, but he was on the ship, as tied to the pursuit as if he had dreamed it up himself. If Ishmael learns anything from his mad ride with Ahab, it is the detective's truth, and the writer's—that no performance is solo, that the one thing you may be sure of is that every human decision, no matter how slight or peculiar, is within reach of every other such decision, as near as Afghanistan. In 2011, we still are in Afghanistan. We are about to hold a presidential election. Call us Ishmael. The street connects us like a hyphen.

SEE FOR YOURSELF. Once in a while in my wanderings, I will pass someone who looks both familiar and strange, as if his face were a concoction of features that at once suggested the categories of physiognomy and his inimitable peculiarity. Such a person could be hailed as a long-lost friend one has never met, but there is no name, no identifying label, for someone like that. Nothing would come of the greeting anyway, unless he had reached the same conclusion about me. I would toss him a warm hello, only to be rebuffed, highhatted. We are so close to being anything but strangers to one another. Yet not so close ever to act on the thought.

In the blazing window of an electronics store on Thirty-second and Lex, eight flat-screen TVs show a Republican presidential debate. All the candidates, including the women, wear dark blue, which makes the line of them look like the sea at night. Their blue line effects a horizon. The women wear colorful scarves, the men wear colorful neckties. As I watch them, a small Latino in a Yankees jacket and a brown wool cap walks up to stand beside me at the window. After a minute, he asks, without turning to me, "What they say?" "Beats me," I tell him. "Beats me," he repeats, as if my answer were a translation.

"TURN DOWN THAT boom box!" I shouted to a group of boys loping down Broadway. I was walking with our children.

"Why do you hate our music?" the boys shouted back.

"I don't hate your music," I said, smiling. "I hate you." They laughed and turned up the volume.

Truth is, I love Latin music. I find it thrilling, though I do not have a Latin bone in my body. But I can play a rumba on the piano, and a samba and a tango. And I can dress up like José Greco, black hat and all, which I did once in a while at home, to no family reactions whatever, not so much as a stare. On the street, whenever Latin music came blaring from a radio, I would improvise a dance. Spin aggressively. Snap my fingers like castanets. Clap my hands above my head. Flamenco me. Mortified again, the children would stage-whisper, "Dad!" and tug at my clothing to make me stop. "You're embarrassing us," they said.

They were right. I ought to have behaved with more decorum. Yet secretly, I think, they enjoyed my dance. And embarrassment is thrilling in its way.

SHIT! MY FATHER did things like that—jumping up from his chair and bleating lines from show tunes, accompanied by a clumsy soft-shoe. Only in his case, these outbursts of entertainment were joyless, as if he were assaulting the silence in his home, which he himself had instituted. Once in a rare while a hapless distant relative, in the city for a couple of days, would call and ask to come over for a visit. He would not have bothered had he known that my father's mind had exiled all his relatives, seen and unseen, beyond Siberia.

One Sunday, my father's nephew, a pleasant gentle young man, phoned asking if he might drop in to say hello. He had just come from Buffalo with his new and happy wife. For over an hour, we made small talk in the living room—all except my father who, in his dark three-piece suit, sat on the bench in front of the bookshelves, saying not a word, even when directly addressed. Instead, in a low and ghostly key, he whistled the entire score of "Wish You Were Here."

WHEN I WAS on my own in the vast apartment, little things drew my attention. A small square inkwell of my father's, in which the black ink had dried on the inside of the glass, effecting a little wall of hieroglyphics. A maroon fountain pen beside it, with a tiny gold lever to draw in the ink. Photographs here and there. My father, mother, and I (age three) sitting on a low stone wall in Chatham, where my parents had rented a sea captain's cottage. My parents strolling on the boardwalk in Atlantic City on their honeymoon—my dad in a black winter coat and a derby, holding a pair of suede gloves in his right hand; my mother in a slim fur coat and heels with bows and a gardenia corsage on her left shoulder. A snapshot of my mother and her sister, Julia, when they were counselors in a summer camp upstate; their flirty smiles. My father at sea in a white suit, on a boat to Honduras, where he served as ship's doctor one summer. He rests his arms on a railing, and looks away.

Faces and figures in the paintings. When my parents first moved into 36, they had nothing to put on the many high walls. They went to Gimbels, which was holding a sale on unpacked crates of hundreds of oils and watercolors, acquired yet never viewed by William Randolph Hearst on one of his manic buying sprees. Among the Hearst artworks in our home was a portrait of a French farmer, with ruddy cheeks and poorly drawn hands; an English landscape showing a boy and girl ascending a hill toward a castle that looked a bit like Leeds; and several moody Italian scenes of decaying structures, walls, and houses, from the late seventeenth century. The canvases were cracked like stale cake. My favorite was that of a dark bridge over a rushing river with alpine mountains in the background and a black leafy tree reaching out over the water like an old man's hand. Fishermen in a canoelike boat examined what looked like corpses covered in sheets.

In a little corner of the bookshelf the radio sat, and I beside it in the late afternoons and early evenings before bedtime—the polished box-cathedral issuing the stories that thrilled my heart. *Mr. and Mrs. North. The Shadow. Boston Blackie. The FBI in Peace and War. The Inner Sanctum. The Green Hornet,* on which the manservant Kato had his nationality changed from Japanese to Filipino immediately after Pearl Harbor. *The Whistler,* which opened with eerie whistling and a portentous voice announcing, "I am the Whistler, and I know many things, for I walk by night." And *Mr. Keen, Tracer of Lost Persons.* All the crime stories presented to me in my corner of the bookshelf. The scary music. The silly music. Mr. Keen's theme song—"Some Day I'll Find You." The Shadow and a tracer of lost persons. "Who knows what evil lurks in the hearts of men?" I curled up like a comma.

While commandeering every surface in the place were ashtrays. Small round glass ashtrays. Square ashtrays, bordered in leather to lend them men's-club elegance. On the side tables, coffee tables, the kitchen table, the dining room table, the dinette table. Fatal furniture. My father smoking cigarettes, cigars, and a pipe. My mother smoking Chesterfields, promoted as the "women's cigarette" after the war, as opposed to manly Camels. Watching the ashes grow longer and longer. Cleaning out the ashtrays, and replacing them, as smoke ghosted through the rooms of the apartment. Smoking in easy chairs, in cars, in offices, in bed. LSMFT, Lucky

Strike Means Fine Tobacco. I'd walk a mile for a Camel. The
Marlboro Man. Old Gold. Ashtrays. Ashtrays. All fall down.

IF YOU GIVE a poor man money, he is bound to look
improved—happier, more alive, more substantial all around.
It is not the same for streets. I approach Fourteenth between
Third Avenue and Union Square East. When I wasn't heading north on my boyhood detecting prowls, I walked down to
Fourteenth. Suspects left and right. Men's clothing stores no
one seemed to shop in; a boxing gym where once I watched
Floyd Patterson work the light bags; a bowling alley, pretty
much of a dive, that sold Yogi Berra's Yoo-hoo chocolate water
drink, and where I brought Ginny on our first high school date
on a snowy night in March. That she took to the place proved
her a gamer. In those days, the alley still employed pin boys,
wizened kids from the poorest areas below Fourteenth Street,
who earned nickels dodging gutter balls. Everything on Fourteenth Street bespoke the life of the run-down. But life.

Today, only the Con Ed building remains unchanged
among business enterprises geared for the upper crust. The
buildings are much bigger, taller, the renovated street merely
a broad aisle for merchandise. On the south side, a P.C. Richard & Son is flanked by two NYU buildings. On the street
level of the NYU building closer to Third is a Trader Joe's
and a separate Trader Joe's Wine Shop. On the street level of

Con Ed is a Raymour & Flanagan furniture store, and across Irving Place from Con Ed, a two-towered apartment house offering a Chipotle restaurant, a Subway sandwich shop, a UPS store, and a Food Emporium, opposite a Walgreens. Brand names of modern America. One may furnish one's apartment in a tower, acquire a Sub-Zero in which to stock food, load up on good wine, get enough Advil and antidepressants to survive the day, seek higher education at night, and never leave Fourteenth Street.

In 1854, on the site of the Con Ed building, the four-thousand-seat Academy of Music opera house was erected, flourishing there till it was taken down in 1926. In 1927, the Academy of Music movie theater was put up across the street, where Trader Joe's is now. It had three thousand seats and tiers of balconies and royal boxes. When the kids of our neighborhood were not heading up to the Loew's Lexington on Fifty-first or west to Eighth Avenue and the RKO on Twenty-third, we came here. My parents took me to Marx Brothers revivals at the Academy of Music when I was five and six. When I was older, I would go by myself. I saw *House of Wax,* the first 3D movie, with Vincent Price. It included a sort of juggler-barker who stood outside the wax museum and promoted it by hitting a rubber ball attached to a paddle by an elastic band. The ball shot straight at the audience. Everyone ducked. The movie was okay as a thriller, but not much of a mystery.

Where the P.C. Richard & Son appliances gleam under fierce lights these days, stood Luchow's, the famous German restaurant, with its sauced-up meats and Oompa Band and big, glorious *tannenbaum* at Christmas. In the 1890s Diamond Jim Brady proposed to Lillian Russell in Luchow's, offering the musical theater star one million dollars if she'd marry him. He brought the money in a suitcase. Russell turned him down. My father said that Luchow's had been a "Nazi hangout" during the war. I tried to picture that—Nazis in uniform lounging around the restaurant, elbows on the bar, just hanging out.

Meanwhile, tonight, the ones who work for a living stoop and lift at a loading ramp at Trader Joe's, hauling cartons on rollers as if they were hauling carts of coal in Pennsylvania or gold in Brazil. They deposit their shadows at the side of the ramp. They are muscular, black, biblical. I have no strength left in my arms. But they could haul a house, a pyramid if they had to. What wouldn't I give, I think as I edge past them on the sidewalk, and they apologize for being in my way. I shrug to indicate that I am in theirs. And then—and such things happen in New York—the tallest one, with a tattoo of lightning on his neck, unbidden in the quickening cold, begins to sing "Someone to Watch Over Me," in a bass so earthy, it seems to rise from the roots of a nearby oak. I stop in my tracks, and listen to the song until the end, when I reach for an imaginary glass and raise it to toast the man.

AND NOW TO Irving Place, which runs six blocks between Fourteenth and Gramercy Park and is changed much less from when I was a kid. This street, too, was created by Samuel Ruggles when he created Gramercy Park. He gave it its name because he liked Washington Irving. He also named Lexington Avenue, to the north of the park, after the Battle of Lexington, which, I suppose, he also liked.

Different stores here now, but located in the same old buildings. A cheese shop where the Sleepy Hollow Book Shop once was, and where my mother bought me children's books. A Japanese restaurant. The Washington Irving High School is here still, a massive place nearly filling the square block between Sixteenth and Seventeenth and Irving Place and Third. At the northeast corner of the building, a big bronze bust of Washington Irving looking wan. The school was all girls when I was a kid, and had a rough reputation. Walking home from school one spring day, I passed a crowd in front of the building, pointing and murmuring. Police kept them back. A teacher, a young man, had jumped or been pushed from the roof, nine stories up. He lay like a slain deer on the pikes of the iron gate around the school, streaks of blood on his brown tweed sports jacket. I had no urge to solve that case.

MURDER. NOTHING LIKE it. All other crimes step aside when the word is spoken. *Murder.* In *Green for Danger* (1946), a nifty mystery movie, a parish nurse interrupts a dance party of doctors and nurses by stopping the phonograph music and announcing from a little balcony above the crowd that a patient's recent death was not due to natural causes, as had been assumed. "It was murder," she says, giving the word all the weight it can bear. *Muurrderr.* She holds the *u* and rolls the *r*'s.

Alfred Hitchcock used it as the title of an early film. Agatha Christie used it all the time—*Murder on the Orient Express, Murder at a Gallop, Murder Most Foul.* I have no idea how it became the collective noun for crows, but think of the image, that cloud of blackness. No word in English has its heart-freezing effect. Speak it, and one does not merely see death, but also the act of killing, and the killer, the weapon, the body, the blood. The better detective writers use it sparingly because of its dreaded power, because murder is the center of human evil, the worst someone can do to someone else.

In *Green for Danger,* Alstair Sim plays the crafty and methodical police inspector, called in on the case after the nurse who pronounced the word at the dance party is murdered herself. Knowing who the murderer is, she runs from the party to the operating theater, to collect the evidence. She hears a noise. The doors to the operating room are flapping on their hinges. She looks up and sees in the limpid light a figure in a white operating gown and mask and cap, covering the face. The figure holds a gleaming knife.

BLOOD. BLOOD IN SYRIA, South Africa, in shopping malls. Blood on college greens. Green blood. *Bang bang bang bang bang.* When I stand at the epicenter of the century's madness (this century or the last), I try not to be deceived by my own sanity. After all, what profiteth a man to be sane in a madhouse? On the other hand, why go crazy with the rest? I can always make it through by speaking of money, because money's where the action is, here at the epicenter. Instead I'd rather listen to you tell me a tale of heroic peoples who did not underestimate their enemies, but understood that shame is real and can stink up a refrigerator, even a Sub-Zero, for a lifetime. On my walk, on anybody's walk, lies the epicenter of the century's madness. Epicenters are quiet places, though they represent the tumultuous.

Thirty years ago, when I was writing for *Time* magazine, I flew over Hiroshima's epicenter in a helicopter I had hired because I wanted to go where the *Enola Gay* had gone after it dropped the Bomb, at the same cruising altitude. A reckless notion. It taught me nothing. And the wind that morning was crazy, the chopper shaking up me and the pilot like a bird in a dog's jaws. This was all in the interests of a cover I was writing on the forty-fifth anniversary of Hiroshima, which *Time* called "My God, What Have We Done." The conventional question, or exclamation, or whatever. They might have called it "The Case of the Disappeared City," though there wasn't much mystery as to who done it.

The difference between that epicenter and the one I tread right now? I'm not sure. Hiroshima's was real, this one's theoretical. But both are both. If you want to get ahead in this world, said my dad, first you have to know what it is you want. We wanted to bomb the shit out of the Japanese and we want to be rich. I ask you, pal: What's so complicated about that?

IN ANY CASE, epicenters are uncomfortable. If I had to choose one place to make my stand, it would not be an epicenter of anything. It would not be a place at all, but rather the midway point between poetry and prose. That is where the best moments of our minds occur, between poetry and prose, our truest selves. Isn't that so? The sweet, solid territory between the two main forms of writing allows for thoughts and feelings not available to each alone. A man may travel to the moon, and at the same time lie curled in his lover's bed. So, at the midway point, we tell a tale of high adventure, and we sing it, too.

By the world we are appalled, and we also sympathize with it. With the world we sympathize, and we also are appalled by it. When we are appalled, we write prose. When we sympathize, we write poetry. But when we wish to get at the truth of the matter, when we want to be honest with ourselves, and with others, we write both.

Archimedes bragged that he could move the world if he had a long enough lever and a place to stand on, with one foot in poetry and the other in prose. Or something like that. Perhaps it's best to write in the ellipses, when there are no words. I should like to live on those three islands, the Ellipses. Ulysses sailed to the Ellipses, I believe.

Do I have that right? In the heart of winter, the old men's season, I listen to Ulysses speaking calmly and judiciously about Scylla and Charybdis, and the Sirens, and the Cyclops, as if they were people of business who simply provided a moment of difficulty for him, a temporary impediment, rather than raising anything life-threatening. To understand him, it may help to remember that it was he who had the brainstorm of a wooden horse, so that the Achaeans could capture Troy. Anyone who can dream up an idea like that needs no help being creative. He might have made it all up—the rocks, the girls, the one-eyed Jack. Of course, there is always the distinct possibility that I may not know my ass from my elbow about any of this. About Ulysses, New York, my work, or you. Or even if I can tell my ass and my elbow apart, I tend toward creative drift myself. Just like Penelope, I lose my thread.

BONG. BONG. BONG. Bong. Bong. Bong. Bong. Atop Met Life is a bell tower, inspired by the freestanding St. Mark's

Campanile in Venice, with clock faces on each of the tower's four sides. The Westminster chimes sound over Gramercy Park. I learned what fifteen minutes meant when I heard the chimes as a child. Also a sense of completeness and incompleteness, as one would wait for all four sets of chimes before hearing the ringing of the new hour. So slow the bells for the new hour. *Bong. Bong. Bong. Bong. Bong. Bong. Bong.*

AND IN CASE you were wondering—because *I* certainly was wondering—this may be as good a place as any to talk about Wallace Stevens's "Tea at the Palaz of Hoon." Not that you ever mentioned the poem. And not that I am at all sure I have the meaning down cold myself. But in spite of all the ellipses in that poem (four-dotters, if there were such a thing), it seems clear that the poem is about the created self. And a boy detective knows something about the created self.

So the idea, I think, is that we live with real people and real events, yet we feel like fictions traveling among them. This is because, while the externalities of our lives remain stable, even adamant, we function in a continual state of self-creation, malleable, fluent. When the Hoon poem states at the end, "I was the world in which I walked," it means that the poet influences the conscious life about him by making an imaginative construction of himself. And that this self, the detective or the writer, though he moves about in "the loneliest air," is hardly lonely. Indeed, he celebrates (privately), because he finds himself, as a result of his illimitable walks, "more truly and more strange."

Yet this is where the detective's and the writer's view of things becomes a bit tricky, because the world the detective observes, while not imagined, has all the thrills of an imagined construct. Holmes means it in "A Case of Identity," when he tells Watson that "life is infinitely stranger than anything which the mind of man could invent." And just when we find ourselves agreeing with Holmes, and rooting for nonfiction over fiction, it comes to us that Holmes is himself a fictional creation. So Conan Doyle is playing us here, but also making a point. Holmes, not real, instructs Watson, not real, in the wonders of reality. The wonder is Holmes himself, the fictional detective in pursuit of a fictional crime that he creates the fiction of solving. Truth is, nothing ever is solved in a Sherlock Holmes story because it never happened. If life is "infinitely stranger" than fiction, how could one ever solve its mysteries?

In any case—and frankly, you can get a fine old headache trying to work out "Tea at the Palaz of Hoon," the very title of which suggests that Stevens intended to give us a headache— the poem is happy. I was the world in which *I* walked. And though I moved through the loneliest air, hardly was I lonely. Not less was I myself. I was more myself. My boy detective. My self-created self. Happy. Fairly happy. In case you were wondering.

I LIKE LIVING my life without telling anyone, as if whatever
I did during the course of a day—get the car an oil change,
shop for coconut ice cream, sit in Starbucks with my grande
bold coffee and yellow legal pad—was between me and me and
no one else. I would not say that what I do is none of your
business. That's not what I mean. Everybody's business is everybody's business once in a while. What I mean is that doing
things like taking a walk in the city at night without telling
anyone makes the thing being done a modest gift to myself. We
live most of our lives this way, do we not? Unnoticed and un-
announced. And who would I tell anyway? Do you really care
if I buy coconut ice cream, or if one winter evening I leave my
classroom and roam about New York in search of my incon-
sequential life? Would you love me more or less if I told you?

TELL US ABOUT yourself, anyway.

Not much to tell.

Tell us anyway.

Look, Lieutenant, I try to cooperate with the police as
much as possible. But I don't see—

Just a few basic facts.

Okay, a few. I play the piano by ear, jazz and pop mainly.
Too lazy to learn to read music. I type with two fingers—one,
really, the index finger on my right hand. The left index I
use for capital letters. I swim with my head completely sub-

merged, not turning it from side to side to breathe, as one is supposed to do. I play tennis by the seat of my pants, running around my backhand to convert it to a forehand. I bank by guessing my balance, keeping whatever I can remember about checks I've written in my head.

You don't!

I do.

Do you get the balance right?

Not even close. In fact, I've never learned to do anything properly except drive a car, which I did by taking lessons from the AAA after failing the road test twice because I was trying to imagine what the rules of the road might be.

What about writing?

I write by ear, too. Oh yes. One other thing I've learned to do correctly is kayaking. I took lessons in kayaking. That's about it, Lieutenant. Are we done?

INSTEAD OF ALL those facts, how about some feeling? Feeling is first, says E. E. Cummings, after all. How I wish I could capture for you that intake of breath on a cloudy Saturday morning, when I had left the gloom of my home behind me, emerged from under the green awning into the leaden air, saluted Carroll the doorman, and started out on my day's adventure. The gashes of sunlight. The poem of the city— every person of every shape, style of dress, and color moving through the stanzas of the streets, each dreaming, in one dream or another, of love or money. A tremendous crime story lay before me, I was certain, a mystery so tangled, monstrous, so full of misleading coincidences, cross-purposes, blind alleys, and the darkest intents, that only the greatest sleuth in the world was capable of seeing into it.

That man there, at the perfume counter in Woolworth's. Wasn't he the one I had spotted two weeks earlier, coming out of the White Castle, wearing a yellow-and-blue plaid scarf and a long black cashmere coat, his hands stuffed hard in the pockets? Only two weeks ago, his hair was blond, not red, and he wore it longer, and his pants weren't creased, and he didn't walk with a limp. But it was the same fellow. I could tell by the ears. As every PI knows, you can change your appearance nearly completely, but never the ears.

The shadow at the base of a brown brick warehouse. The tunnels of alleys. The clip of footsteps. A hallway lit in silver. The ruins of a church. A slash of light from a window with the shades drawn. And then the shade rises. A hand. A patch of imagined gaslight. A lost letter lifted by the wind. A startled look of recognition as a stranger hustles past, then turns around halfway down the block at the very moment you turn around, and you both know something you will never tell anyone else.

Not in so many words did I tell myself that such mornings offered the best of life to me, but the evidence was all around me. Not in so many words did I understand that life was dark and wild, and that it insisted you look at it, pry into it, and face it with equal amounts of suspicion and affection. But who could not see this was so? I knew who I was, but I could not say it. Not in so many words. Yet, as I learned eventually, when words became the coins of my realm, how many words does it take?

IN GENERAL, LESS was said when I was a child. More was implied. Perhaps because there were commonly shared as-sumptions about things, both good and bad, or because people knew "their place" and everyone knew everyone else's place, which also was good and bad. But for one reason or other, less was said. Detectives never talk a lot anyway. You never met a detective who runs off at the mouth. Detective Chief Super-intendent Christopher Foyle of the British TV series *Foyle's War*, which is set during the Second World War, for instance, never used a word that didn't count. Such a good writer.

I don't know that people did more thinking simply because they did less talking. One thing, though: Speaking less allowed for fewer careless outbursts, thus creating at least a veneer of civilization. The abrupt nod of the head. In my childhood I saw so many men, in particular, give one another abrupt nods that seemed to convey a good deal more than a mere greeting or agreement. Don't see many these days. The nod that seemed to be worth a thousand words has been replaced by them.

Detective Chief Superintendent Foyle had a habit of nodding just before he quietly clobbered someone with a devastating piece of information, which often revealed that person's culpability. He would go straight to the point. He would say "Right," meaning "Wrong." He would say "No. You're lying." I miss the world where people said "No. You're lying." Sometimes Foyle would just raise an eyebrow.

And all this emerged from a sense of justice, a font of justice, because the detective we most admire and honor is imbued with justice and is not simply assigned to see that justice is done. He must not only think justice is right. He must not only believe that civilization depends on its enactment. Justice must flow in his microbes and genes, so that when he goes after a bad guy or arrests him, he is satisfying something essential in his own makeup. In truth, he could no more live without justice than without air or water. I am thinking of all of them, the best of them. Holmes, Maigret, Poirot, Marple, Lord Peter Wimsey, Philo Vance, Marlowe, Spade, Archer, Wolfe. But here on this walk of mine, I am thinking especially of Foyle, who, even after he retired from the police department, could not let an injustice stand, particularly as it involved the weak. In the last episodes of *Foyle's War,* the war is over, and crime is not officially Foyle's business. Yet he pursues unfairness, cowardice, and bigotry for no other reason than that they must be pursued. Foyle was not merely a policeman. He was a man. His job, his position in the world, was that of being a man. What child would not wish to grow up to be Detective Chief Superintendent Foyle? What child with a nose for crime?

HERE'S HOW NOSY I could be: When I was six, my parents rented a small summerhouse in Westport, Connecticut, on a leafy street. It came with a collie named Lady, which was great for me because our own dog had died the previous winter. On the first day there, as my parents unpacked, I took a stroll down the new street and came to a large Tudor house with a glass-walled sunroom in the back. Peering in, I saw a gleaming concert grand. The door was open, so I walked in, just like that, and I began to play "Danny Boy" and "The Blue Danube," the two pieces I had picked out some months earlier. As I played, a blonde in her twenties, who looked like a princess in a fairy tale, entered from the main house, stood at the far end of the piano, and gently smiled. She listened to me play, gave me cookies, took me back to my parents, and told them the story of my bold visit. She called it remarkable. My parents came up with another word.

Has anyone seen Dr. Teucher lately—he who, during that summer in Westport, took out his .22 pistol and shot kittens in his basement? One night I heard the shots. If you crossed the street to Dr. Teucher's home, and looked past the Bilco doors into the dark, you could see the kittens lying on their sides in blood and fur. Their eyes were closed. Four, seven, maybe twelve. "Why did Dr. Teucher do that, Dad?" My father made a grim smile. "Too many kittens, I guess," he said.

Our second summer in Connecticut, Peter had been born. My parents rented a house in Weston, a farm community then. No neighbors in sight. My father commuted to the city and remained for two, three weeks at a time. My mother stayed with my brother, sometimes in the garden, mostly indoors. That marked the beginning of her long retreat into caring for Peter, and away from my father, and from me. A few years later, I read about a comedian, Jack Douglas, who had written a bestseller called *My Brother Was an Only Child*. I got the joke.

In Weston, I rode my bike for miles every day, past hayfields, pastures, and orchards, meeting no one and looking for crime. Holmes always thought the worst crimes were committed not in the city, but in this brooding quietude of the countryside, the dead calm. Yet it's hard to spot crime in a rural setting unless you're Agatha Christie or Dorothy Sayers. The whorls of birds. The shadows of horses. Returning to the house one late afternoon, I saw a patrol car in the driveway, and my mother with a policeman. She was flapping her arms and, in her quiet way, shouting. My father had driven off and a copperhead had been coiled under his car. By the time the police arrived, it had disappeared. I went snake hunting in the tall dry grass.

I DON'T KNOW a lot about nature, but I know what I like—
the feeling of impersonal companionability in the countryside, walking in the woods or fields. Trees tilting at slight
angles like cowhands on a break, birds wheeling in the wind,
all of nature leading a life independent from your own, yet involved with it by implication. At the age of three, in Chatham,
when I would wander away from my parents' cottage, I never
felt any fear, though nature towered over me. Only comfort.
At *Time,* I wrote a series on people who had accomplished
heroic things for the environment. I visited a rain forest in
Suriname that was dazzling with its red ants, howler mon-
keys, and bright-colored toads. Nature putting on a show. Yet
I've always felt more at home in the less dramatic places, such
as the New England woods, which is a marketplace of small
activities—caterpillars and beetles going about their business
as you go about yours.

   In his *Confessions,* Tolstoy admitted that as a small child
he knew next to nothing about nature. He assumed he must
have been privy to flowers and leaves, yet up to his fifth or
sixth birthday, he had no memory of the natural life. This
separation he calls "unnatural," because he was aware of it,
implying that to be away from nature is to yearn for it un-
consciously. The separation is akin to a separation from one's
passions—from love, from family, from one's very senses.

   Most of city life is separated from nature, and citizens,
aware of the penalties, seek compensations. No one can imag-

ine New York without Central Park, which makes the auto-
cratic decisions of its chief imaginer and builder, Frederick
Law Olmsted, all the more remarkable. In 1857, Olmsted and
his partner, Calvert Vaux, could picture 843 acres of green-
ery, fountains, and footbridges in the midst of the farms and
run-down villages that constituted that area of the city, as well
as picturing a future of suffocating steel towers. It is as if, by
foreseeing the centrality of their park, they were looking into
their own hearts.

Yet, this distant friendship of nature's is like the city's
friendship, too. A walk in the Village or up Madison seems
much like a walk in Vermont in that you feel part of your
surroundings without committing yourself to them. You are
aware of the bees and of your fellow citizens in casual and
indirect ways. I suppose you're also alert to the fact that an
enemy, a mugger or a wolf, can materialize at the drop of a
hat. But the presiding feeling is simply that of being with your
world, and it with you. And there is nothing either of you
wishes to do about it but live and wonder.

GRAMERCY PARK HAD its local naturalist in Theodore
Roosevelt, whose town house stood on Twentieth Street, between Park and Broadway. My mother took me to the Theodore Roosevelt Museum dozens of times before Peter was
born, always, it seemed, on rainy days. The museum is easy

to miss, tucked like an afterthought inside what was a block of wholesale houses when I was young, and now is squeezed, like the Little House of the children's story, between a Realtor called New York Living Solutions and a bar called No Idea, affording both the accurate and evasive answer, I suppose, to the accusing question of an angry spouse: Where *are* you?

So quiet, the home of the wild man president, he of the Rough Riders and Mount Rushmore and the blank goggle eyes and the grillelike teeth. In fact, the museum is not his original home, but rather a reconstruction of the house he was born in, on October 7, 1858. Here he lived till he was fifteen. The museum stands exactly where his home did, before it was demolished in 1916. The newer house was rebuilt in 1919, funded by prominent New Yorkers who wanted TR to have a proper monument.

So the rooms of the museum are as they were between the years 1865 and 1872. I used to go about inspecting the zebra skin on the wall, the tiger skin rug, the full-size taxidermy lion standing on a pedestal. Mounted heads of wild boar, antelope, and mountain sheep. A glass cabinet contained an eyeglass case with a bullet hole in it, which would catch the attention of any detective. A would-be assassin had taken a potshot at TR in Milwaukee, in 1912. He was saved by his own poor eyesight. Victorian dark, the house. Rugs dark green and maroon, black chairs stuffed with horsehair. The stairs creaked as they did in *The Spiral Staircase*. There were chandeliers once gaslit, like the one in *Gaslight*. My eyes widened at everything in the place.

TR's dad gave the boy a shotgun when he was eleven. The old Abercrombie & Fitch ideal of manhood. I could picture him at my age, his imagination impelling him up and down the staircase, in and out of the rooms. "Charge!" The cry of San Juan Hill. "Charge!" The cry of the nutcase old man in *Arsenic and Old Lace,* who kept popping up from the basement yelling "Charge!" But TR was only part nutcase. To be sure, he built the Panama Canal by stealing Panama from Colombia, and there was all that loony rough-riding. But he also started the Pure Food and Drug Administration, enacted the first child labor laws, and set up the national parks, which made him our first environmentalist president. Let's just say he was conflicted—part do-gooder, part do-badder, a tough case to crack. His first wife and his mother died on the same day, Valentine's Day.

One photograph in the museum showed TR as a boy about my age then, with shiny blond hair and wearing a formal little jacket. Another showed him at age eight, looking out of a window on Union Square at Lincoln's funeral cortege. Never would I have served as a sidekick to any other detective, but I gladly would have been his, at least while we both were children. My fearless playmate, both of us lost in gallant fantasies.

But now I see my mother signaling that it is time to leave,

and the two of us, our separate tours complete, smiling to each other at the museum door, proceed to walk home in the rain.

IT DIDN'T NEED to be TR. I would have been happy with any worthy friend and partner, but I never had one. Guys I knew, and they knew me, and we were friends in the casual sense of the word. What I longed for was a real cohort, someone with whom to follow suspects or write songs or put on plays, an imaginative mind to keep company with my own and to abet and improve my imagination with his. Detectives sometimes have partners, like Sam Spade's Miles Archer, whose murder drives the moral issue of the story, but who, when it comes down to it, was just another name painted on the glass of the door, easily scraped off. That's not the sort of partner I had in mind. I wanted someone to share wonder and bright days with, and burdens, too, I guess, though the thought of sharing my burdens with another person also seemed unfair, since everyone has enough of his own. Shoulder to shoulder. Like a teammate in basketball, and you never have to look where he is on the court, because you know where he is and where he will be—in position for a look-away pass.

In college I found such a friend in Peter Weissman. I knew exactly where he would be on the court, and I know it to this day. Then, we did write songs and plays together, and we played on the same teams, and we laughed at the same nonsense. It would have been especially good to have known Pete in the detective years—to begin each open day with the question "What shall we do now?" And while asking that same question to myself as I went it alone had its many rewards, wouldn't it have been satisfying to have someone with you who could come up with an adventurous answer.

A child went forth every day, and the first object he looked upon, that object he became. So every day I looked upon the park and became the park, the first object I saw in the morning and the last I saw at night. The gated garden of my heart greeted its counterpart. The smudge that passed for my soul arranged itself to accommodate self-satisfied statues and orderly people. And the patches of lawn. A stone urn here and there. The obligations. The savage courtesies. And in the middle, a prisoner tree reaching up and out for sunlight. Warden, we can't eat this food. Hey! What do you know! I'm going to get off scot-free. I'm going to walk.

AND SO WE WALK—up and down the avenues, past the city's vertical villages, where most of the people do most of the living. "The celestial ennui of apartments." That is how Wallace Stevens saw them. And here they are, layer after layer of apartments, and the turmoil therein, and the schemes, the celebrations, the resolve and remorse. But ennui? I don't know. The woman in *King Kong* who was sleeping, minding her own business, when the ape reached in and snatched her out of her bed and tossed her to her death, random, casual. The woman in the dark nightgown. Was that ennui? Hardly. In the older apartment houses around Gramercy Park, and on lower Fifth, each apartment seems a drawer in a jewel box, solid and intact. In the newer buildings, the apartments seem to move laterally, as if they were light shows shuffling and sliding between and away from one another. Paper thin walls. The TVs blast color in high definition, more clearly defined than in life. I look straight up to observe the humming hive, but tonight Visigoths seem to have raided the fortress and no life is on display. Only one man, alone on a penthouse balcony.

Have you read Ray Bradbury's "There Will Come Soft Rains"? The story's title comes from a poem by Sara Teasdale, and both pieces are about the end of the world brought about by people's self-destructive impulses. In Bradbury, a California house is shown with all its machines turned on and working, but the people have disappeared. Maybe that's what happened to this apartment house tonight. A limited nuclear holocaust.

Or the residents may be lying down, so I cannot see them from my vantage point on the street. My voyeur's vantage point. They may be screwing or sleeping. And they remain celestial in Stevens's heaven, until that hairy hand, the size of a barn, reaches in the window, plucks them from the sheets, and flings them, nightgown and all, into my waiting arms.

AS FOR THE man standing at the waist-high Plexiglas wall of the penthouse balcony, he appears to track the stars, but he is thinking of her. She has been asleep since eight. She sleeps a great deal lately, heavy with painkillers. Her voice is faint, like someone heard through a wall. He makes attempts to soothe her. It'll be okay, he tells her. OK. OK. In a few months we'll be driving up to Connecticut again, taking the boat out. He used to believe himself when he said things like that.

Now he thinks of the penthouse apartment behind him, all twelve rooms dark. He wonders how much bigger it will seem when she goes. He wonders how it would have been if they had had children, if he should get a smaller apartment in the same building, or on the other side of town, or in another town, or if he will remarry. He thinks he will get an apartment on a lower floor, nearer the street.

A story he never read, by Dino Buzzati, involves a hospital where the least serious cases are assigned to the top floor and the most serious cases, those expected to die, are assigned to the floor on the ground level. Buzatti's story is about a man who enters the hospital suffering from a mild case of flu, and who is assigned to the topmost floor. But soon something goes wrong with the plumbing on that floor, and so the man is asked if he would mind moving down a floor. On that floor they find there are not enough beds, so again the man is forced to move down. This pattern recurs, floor after floor, until the man who entered the hospital with the flu lies motionless on the lower level, gravely ill.

She coughs twice, then three times, then is quiet again. He remains unmoving on the penthouse balcony. He does not turn his head. In a kind of chorus, like a chant, the rooms of the apartment call his name. They say, we will miss you when you both are gone. You were kind to us, generous. It was good to have you around. But perhaps it is all for the best. The penthouse probably was too big for you, too much for just the two of you, you and the missus.

GLASS PUNCH BOWL of a night. I step across an oil slick that easily might be mistaken for a small puddle, when I am less alert. But something about tonight, the cold, sharpens one's senses. I detect the moon where it attempts to hide behind four black mules who (Godknowshow) have trudged up there beside it. When I approach the Dutch doors of a garbage can, I do not enter. But, on a night like this, that is my choice. On a night like this, I have a heart for everything, including, especially, you. To say nothing of the Holy Ghost and the duck (from the fable of the same name) at the rectory connected with the

Church of the Transfiguration, known as the "Little Church around the Corner," at Twenty-ninth Street, which has been around since 1849 and yet has just gone up before my eyes in a confusion of snowflakes. So, to say nothing of it, I won't.

WHO COULD TIRE of New York? Dr. Johnson said that anyone who tires of London tires of life. *London?* Was he kidding? The roses in the window of an old bar and grill. The stick marks on the sidewalk made when the cement was still wet. The courage of small birds. The courage of people coming from work, going to work. Sometimes, when I drive in from Long Island, before teaching, I pull off to the side, stop, and watch. I close the car windows and put on a CD of John Lewis of the Modern Jazz Quartet, playing a souped-up version of Bach. Or I play the Rach Three, so that my fellow citizens may go about their errands to the accompaniment of Rachmaninoff. The Rach Three moves as they move, alternately melancholy, sprightly, sweet, bittersweet, aggressive, bombastic, sad, and exultant. How brave are these people. Rachmaninoff weeps without tears.

The city does not exist without people walking in it. Does not exist, I say. And if you doubt me, recall those scenes in science fiction movies that attempt to show the end of the world. For the scenes to be persuasive, the cameras do not go to the mountains or to the seashore, both of which can do quite well without human company. Show the Rockies as they would look after a nuclear blast, and the picture would be no different from an ordinary spring day. But when the moviemakers seek to indicate total and absolute lifelessness, they shoot the empty city, and it's almost always New York. Deprived of people, the place is lunar. The buildings look lost. The empty streets look lost. Where people once defined the space, merely by walking here and there, space no longer is.

This is strange, is it not? People walking create the space in which they walk. The walk lays out its own street. Does this mean that when the walkers are removed, the city itself no longer exists? That the space they defined is unreal? And if that is so, no wonder the city feels like a dream. Why, man, it is a dream. I told you so.

See there, pal? If you blur your vision, the soldiers' uniforms become their wars. And instead of merely watching the soldiers on leave as they walk here on Eighteenth and Broadway, you see them in dangerous territories where they earn their stripes, riding in armored MRAPs, in olive, yellow, and brown places where the natives plant IEDs in their path. Not camouflaged in front of Paragon sporting goods, they stand out in a crowd. Earlier, when I passed her, I should have saluted. Even if she blushed or rushed to get by, I should have saluted for the very patch of land that became her uniform. Even if she giggled.

'TIS OF THEE, my country, that I sing, feeling in love with it as ever yet estranged these days, removed from politics and policies, more than when we were in Vietnam, more than when we were in Cambodia, out of it, like a guy suddenly flush, who jiggles the change in his pocket, looking for someone to give it to, and finding no takers, shrugs.

I was in Cambodia, too, not in it exactly but next door, at the Khao I Dang refugee camp in southern Thailand, on another case, talking to children who had escaped Pol Pot's work camps. Some had buried their parents, digging with their little hands. Many had been tortured. In the refugee camp they danced the water drop dance to entertain the visiting journalists. Outside the tent rose a small Golgotha of prosthetic limbs. The weather was inclement. The rain would explode, soaking us from top to bottom, clothing clinging to our bodies. And just when you thought you might go under and drown, the sun would blast the rain away and drape you in a dry heat. You stood where you had stood, unwrinkled as you were before the rains. I felt at home there. Awake. Alive.

America is a detective story, is it not? It runs from hope to crime to pursuit to justice to regeneration, and back to hope. I've always had a special taste for the beginnings of detective stories, when we come upon our hero, who is either glum and disheveled or elegant and cocky, doing nothing but waiting to be called into action. He receives a client. Or the cops need his help. Off he goes, from crime to pursuit to justice to regeneration. But before all that, oh! That first blush of hope, when the case is laid before him like the shores before the sailing ships, and the promise of adventure and decency and virtue is as innocent as daylight. Our private eye has been engaged to solve the most pressing, important problem in the world. He is Einstein. He is Darwin. Once he accomplishes his mission, nothing ever will be the same. He is Columbus.

WHAT IF THEY had fallen off the flat earth? The early explorers, I mean, who were afraid their tall ships would fall off the flat earth if they sailed to what they supposed was a new world, but sailed anyway, thinking what have we got to lose? Wild men, crazy men, desperados, cutthroats. How could it not be worth a high-stakes gamble for lowlife like that? A chance at riches, homes of their own in a paradisiac place, with a native woman, perhaps, naked from the waist up, red flowers in her hair, black comforting eyes. A second chance at life, just like Lazarus. Who would not risk falling off the flat earth for such a payoff?

But what if, in fact, they had fallen off the earth, which, as they had feared, was flat as a pancake—their great sails ballooned with wind, plowing straight ahead and then straight down, as if they'd tumbled from a kitchen shelf, into night forever? Imagine that, won't you, as I recall an astronomy professor who gave a lecture at the Smithsonian some years ago, about a mystery concerning the human race. He stood at one end of the stage holding an orange, which he called the sun. Then he walked to the other end, holding a speck of dust, which he called the earth. He stood silent for a moment before saying, as if to himself: "Either we are alone in the universe, or we are not alone. I find both propositions equally unbelievable." By the way, did you know that the word *planet* derives from the ancient Greek verb *planasthai,* meaning "to wander"? Well, there you go.

To return to the hypothesis then: What if the early explorers had fallen off the flat earth instead of discovering the round earth, with all that went along with that discovery—the riches, the homes, the native women with the bare breasts and the comforting eyes? What if they fell and disappeared, and thus we had disappeared before we got started, you and I, and everything disappeared, and nothing was ever heard again of the new world, because there was no new world. Nothing. Either we fall off the flat earth, or discover a world that goes round and round indefinitely. I find both propositions equally unbelievable.

PAUL MULDOON WONDERED how Europe felt when America left her, calling Europe a grass widow. That's nice. The mere thought raises sentimental possibilities, not the least of which is that nations, or entire continents for that matter, are capable of longing. John Donne would have liked that thought, especially in those moments when he was packing the stars into his love affairs. Big into little. Little into big. In Gramercy Park, the caretakers used to hoist the American flag on the tall white flagpole in the morning, and fold it properly in triangles at night, when it was lowered. The same ritual took place at summer camp, when a counselor played "Reveille" on his bugle at dawn, and "Taps" at night. Not sure why my thoughts go from Muldoon to summer camp. But if Europe did long for us after our departure, the longing could have gone the other way round, I suppose, us for them. But it didn't.

European explorers return home. American explorers keep walking. That, in a nutshell, is the difference between European and American explorers. And, come to think of it, between Europe and America.

HERE'S A THOUGHT: If there were a place on earth that no one had ever been, would you go there? Those explorers did that all the time. They congratulated themselves for going places where no one had ever traveled, same as E. E. Cummings, who wrote, "Somewhere I have never travelled," referring to a different sort of trip. But these days, is it possible to find a place where no one has been, not a soul? They speak of desert islands—"If you could be on a desert island with just one book . . ."—the assumption being that once there, that's it, and you are stuck for a lifetime in a place to which no ship will sail, and where no one has been, or ever will be, but you. You and your one book. My question is that if such a place existed would you be drawn to it?

It's absurd, I know. But I feel that way about certain streets in my territory, where I never have wandered before, not as a boy, not ever. How could it be that I who have covered so much ground, never walked down Thirty-first between Park and Lex? I don't know what was here years ago, but today some unusual colonists have settled the block—Jews for Jesus, the Hai-Lan Chinese American Cultural Society, the Sukyo Mahikou Center for Spiritual Development, and Murray Hill Comedy Hours. Many thousands have walked here before, I am sure, but since this street is new to me, it becomes my Florida, my Mars. So I tread carefully, with much curiosity. What language do they speak here? What are the mores? Tell you what. Let's build a new civilization on this spot, you and I, and replace the comedy club and Jews for Jesus with shimmering temples and great golden domes and stuff like that, a brand-new start that ensures ourselves of eternal ecstasy for everyone. No. I'm not mad. Well, maybe. A little.

IF I WERE—mad, that is—I'd choose the madness of George C. Scott in *They Might Be Giants,* a favorite movie of boy detectives. The title comes from Don Quixote tilting at windmills. Scott plays a wealthy former judge thought mad by his family because he believes himself to be Sherlock Holmes, wears a deerstalker, and pursues evil. The family, wanting his money, plans to have Scott locked up in a mental hospital. The psychiatrist they engage, played by Joanne Woodward, is named Mildred Watson, so Dr. Watson is supposed to certify Holmes's madness.

But, as it turns out, Watson falls in with Holmes, and then in love with him, not because he is or is not crazy, but rather because his mad pursuit is just. Throughout the movie, Scott goes after Moriarty, the embodiment of evil. In the end, his family is thwarted and evil is confronted. After a wild chase through the city, Holmes faces Moriarty, who reveals himself as a blinding light. The supreme detective engages the supreme enemy on the streets of New York. When that light filled the screen, I gasped.

HOWEVER TERRIFYING AND dismaying madness is to those who come in contact with it, still it may be mesmerizing to a child. When I was eight or so, I used to listen to Mrs. Antonetti, dressed in her nightclothes, walk up the marble stairs at the back of number 36, crying out for her baby daughter, Mary. At the time, Mary was a grown woman living in another state, but Mrs. Antonetti had it in her head that her child was still an infant, living with her on the third floor, and she searched for her on the back stairs. "Oh that Mary Antonetti," she wailed. "Oh that Mary Antonetti. She's always leaving home."

One night, I heard her wailing and I peeked out the back door of our apartment. I wanted to see Mrs. Antonetti, though I also was afraid of her. So I stood on the ninth-floor landing and listened as she ascended toward me, flight after flight. As her voice grew louder and more plaintive, I wanted to retreat into the apartment. But Mrs. Antonetti, rising in my direction, her bedroom slippers scuffling on the marble stairs, her cries coming closer, held me entranced.

She was on the seventh floor, then the eighth, and now she approached the ninth, and me. "Oh that Mary Antonetti. She's always leaving home." Finally, she reached where I was standing, and looked me over, unstartled. Her hair was disheveled, and her eyes were tired. "Have you seen my Mary?" she asked. Too frightened to speak, I stood my ground. She made her way around me and proceeded to the tenth floor, disappearing where the stairs took a turn. Her voice echoed like an ambulance siren in the hall. I remained transfixed. I understood nothing about Mrs. Antonetti or her hopeless quest, except perhaps that not every tunnel has a light at the end of it.

NO LIGHT HERE. He gropes her in an alley off Twelfth Street, between Fifth and University Place. He gropes her between Fifth and University. Well, not exactly an alley, more like a slot between two 1920s brownstones. He gropes her in the slot. And she gropes back, the two explorers like stalks of corn, vertical, rocking, oblivious of me. I ought to be oblivious of them, discreet, even if they are not. But, as the saying goes, I can't take my eyes off them, just as they can't take their hands off each other. It isn't easy, their groping. They have to excavate each other under the layers of winter clothing. Their breathing makes clouds.

Elizabeth Bishop has a poem about the mechanical nature of lovemaking, called "Edgar Allan Poe & the Juke-Box," though it is not exactly about that. It is about being exact. It wonders if sexual pleasures, being mechanical, are premeditated. Or do they just come, as the two in the alley are about to? And what does Poe (who seems to pop up everywhere on this walk) have to do with all that—poor Edgar, who is dragged into every human strangeness, including the effects of jukeboxes upon sexual mores. Well, I suppose he asked for it, after "Marie Rogêt" and the rest. Detective Poe walks the streets downtown, passes the room with the jukebox, and plays a tune. In for a nickel.

THE BEST DAYS are the first to flee, said Virgil. But before they do . . . The birthday party when I was six, and, after blowing out the candles, singing every word of "Blue Skies" for my small bewildered guests. At age four, sitting at the concert grand beside enormous Miss Jourdan, the editor and novelist, who lived upstairs with Miss Prescott, the Columbia University librarian, and Miss Cutler, the ceramicist. Accompanying my dad on rounds, and winding up at the counter at the drugstore on Twentieth and Park, the two of us hunched over ham sandwiches and black-and-white sodas. Tracking earthworms in the park. Riding an inner tube in Long Island Sound, straight to Portugal. Pears in a wooden crate. A horse's neck, as he is about to take a jump. The sea captain's house in Chatham, with the ship's wheel in the living room. Snow piled like frosting on my bedroom windowsill. A road under a hard blue sky, and, though you cannot see it or smell the brine, the sea it leads to.

And my mother, having returned home from teaching junior high English in a school on Hester Street. And her mother, Sally, lounging around our gothic museum in the late afternoons while I, the apple of their eyes, deployed brightly painted British soldiers in the Charge of the Light Brigade on the green bedroom carpet. My grandmother, whom I called Giga, big face, black hair, singing "Look for the Silver Lining." And my mother brandishing a shawl, strutting around the bedroom, like Mae West.

And taking walks with her in the neighborhood, to the TR Museum, or the Gramercy Bakery with its odor of lemon meringue, and the Gramercy Florist and the cold air of roses, and the milliner on Twenty-second Street. A felt suede crown. A blue feather.

And my mother's father, Joachim, whom I called Patta, getting off the Third Avenue El, and coming to our house from his sign-painter shop in the Bronx, and sitting at the end of my bed to tell me stories. I was five. And the night he sat there saying nothing, and I waited eagerly until finally he said in his pea-soup accent, "This time, *you* tell *me* a story." And I: "But, Patta, I don't have a story to tell." And he: "Tell me something you did today."

So I told him about Mr. Platt, who took a bunch of the neighborhood kids to Palisades Park that afternoon, and all the wonderful rides we went on, and the go-carts, and the Ferris wheel and the waterfall, and the little pond, which I stretched to the size of a lake, and the live alligator with two teeth, one gold, one silver, that chased me up a hill into a cave where I hid beside a black bear, the two of us sitting very quietly, burying our faces in cardboard cones of cotton candy. And I saw Patta's look of amused attentiveness, in which I also saw the power of words. And I loved what I saw.

WHAT DID WE know back then, you and I, of treachery and lies? It was white, all whiteness, and we stood waist high in the new snow, glancing up at the laden boughs, also white, and at the whitened houses of the imperiled birds. Some days, I picked out blues on the piano. Some days, I just sang. I don't mean once, or just one song, but a long time, much of the day.

I sang "Bye Bye Blackbird" and "Molly Malone" and sang da, da, da to "Peter and the Wolf," all the animals. Some days, I sat on the window seat in the living room and whistled. Some days, I sat at the kitchen window and dug into the sill. Some days, I played canasta with the three ladies upstairs, who, on other days, read me *Tom Sawyer* and *The Wind in the Willows*. Some days, I smeared saddle soap on my fielder's glove and wrapped it with leather straps. Some days, I led a cavalry charge, with you at my side, pal.

Hard to believe there was time left for anything else, such as the sneer or the sidelong glance, or the smirk one did not see but rather heard, somehow, between the nodes of the music and the membranes of light. My mother's arms cradling groceries and flowers, and I smiling like a bright idea when she reentered the cave.

It's hard enough loving everyone, including the beasts of the school years and the petty criminals who have tried to stain every step of your life, without having to write beautiful things for the multitudes, and wishing them well in the bargain. The trouble with love when sold as cough medicine is that it can stick in your throat like a fishbone. You really have to believe what you say through and through. I mean, who the fuck can do that?

But this is Thirty-fourth Street, where B. Altman's used

to be, with the birdcage in front of the restaurant called The Birdcage, and a white-haired hag pushes a grocery cart of vague possessions before her as she crosses at the red, causing a city bus to hiss to a stop, not to mention the cursing cars, and the furious cop—while she, self-contained as you please, doesn't give a shit. Who could not love her?

DETECTIVE, WRITER. Writer, detective. I tell the story of my grandfather as if he urged me on my way. But I don't think it's so. More likely, students, it is one of those memories we find to create patterns and connections in our lives where none exist. In the sixth grade, I wrote a poem about George Washington saying good-bye to his troops. This was not in response to an assignment. I simply was moved to do it. And I wrote things for the school literary magazine, only one of which I recall—a monologue spoken by a lawyer who had deliberately given little effort to his defense of a kid from the streets, because his client represented a lower social class. Pretty obvious stuff.

But actually becoming a writer? I think I was more impressed by the idea of a person who worked alone and did what he liked. I relished stories about writers, movies about writers, as I did about detectives. The very word thrilled me—*writer,* one who imagines all of experience and creates it again. All the world sits in awe of writers, I believed, the storytellers of the race. Best of all, a writer is invisible. He tracks you down without your knowing he's there. And he's *not* there. A book is published. The writer does not have to accompany it. Go, litel bok.

UP AND FARTHER up, I climbed the bookshelves in the living room. I would take off from the bookshelf bench, step onto the second shelf, and begin my ascent—up past the long sets of books, purchased by my parents mainly to fill the shelves. Sets of Dickens, Longfellow, Hawthorne. A set of John Greenleaf Whittier, pale green and brown, bound in a tweedlike fabric. A set of Kipling with suede covers and little swastikas, Indian symbols, on the bindings. Emerson, Austen, Thackeray. The contents of the books meant nothing to me, of course, but as artifacts, they carried mysteries. Up to Turgenev. Across to Balzac. Over to Thoreau. Up and farther up, to the shelf near the top containing the set of orange Childcraft books, which had things for grown-ups to read to children, poems and nursery rhymes, and children's projects. A volume on drawing. A volume on health. And on the inside covers a drawing of a perfectly civilized boy and girl with a butterfly between them. One book had several pages devoted to the construction of a violin. Did they expect a child to do that? Up and farther up. Balancing my little feet in the spaces between where the books were aligned and the shelves ended. And at last there, at the top, where I could plant my hand against the ceiling, twelve feet off the ground, and look down on my mother rocking Peter, and not even knowing I was in the house.

YOU ASK ABOUT the house? The house is everything to a good mystery, be it the grand country manor where the weekend party occurs (see Christie's *Murder for Christmas*, A. A. Milne's *The Red House Mystery,* or Margery Allingham's *Police at the Funeral*), or the hut, or the trailer, or your place. Members of the household are prime suspects. (Did the butler ever do it? Why would you have a butler do it?) It is the house that contains the seethings and the loathings and resentments that end in murder. Someone creeps about the house. The body is discovered in the house, in the pantry, in the library. To the house the detective comes, an inspector calls, the intruder in the house who will shake up the inhabitants and rattle the cage.

The body is discovered in the library. Yes. How often that occurs, as if the authors of mysteries instinctively are drawn to locate the murders in the room closest to their hearts. Nearly always in the great creepy old mystery movies of the 1930s and 1940s a library is shown, with floor-to-ceiling shelves spilling over with misshapen volumes rising to an indoor mist. In a cracked leather chair slumps the body, positioned by the killer to make it look like a suicide. A quick inspection, and the detective can see it wasn't a suicide, could not have been a suicide. The angle of the shot is all wrong. The entry point of the bullet far too high. And the gun was in the victim's left hand.

All this started in England with a real case of murder, in 1860, called the Road Hill case. A three-year-old boy was found mutilated, the body stuffed down the hole in an outhouse on the grounds of a country estate in Wiltshire. The suspects were the inhabitants, family and servants. A history of insanity there. The press clamored for justice, but the police got nowhere until Inspector Jonathan Whicher—one of the first members of the London detective force—was called in. Basing his hypothesis on the missing nightdress of one of the dead boy's half-sisters, he named her the killer, and he was proved right. Yet the public reviled him. How could a murderous child reside in the domestic sanctum, the place of safety, where all good people live? The house.

The Road Hill murder initiated what Wilkie Collins called "a detective fever" in England and elsewhere. *The Moonstone* (1868) was full of facts gleaned from the Road Hill case, though Collins watered down his story, substituting a jewel thief for a murderer. People became enthralled with the pure puzzles of murder cases, perhaps because they proved to be so close to home, and all the fictional cases that followed (Marple, Holmes, and the others) had Road Hill as their point of departure. Whicher himself gave birth to the laconic, ordinary-seeming detective—Collins's Sergeant Cuff, Chandler's Marlowe—whom no one notices until it is too late.

Still, the most lasting legacy of the case was the house. It constituted a world of close relationships in which anything could happen, especially something terrible, in close quarters. See the country house in Henry James's *The Turn of the Screw,* and the governess and the impassive children imprisoned within. See it there at dusk, looming on a hill, its windows blazing, the great front door shut tight. Black clouds settle over the fields behind the gabled roof of the silent house.

You ask about the dog? "Asta!" Myrna Loy's sexy-patrician voice admonishing the famous terrier of Nick and Nora Charles. Movie audiences first met Asta when he was stretching his leash taut, dragging Mrs. Charles into a chichi bar, where Mr. Charles, William Powell, was setting up a row of dry martinis. The dog appeared in subsequent *Thin Man* movies, generally playing more cute than heroic, though he barked to protect the Charles's baby in one of the films. Few detectives have dogs. Philo Vance, a breeder of Scottish terriers, owned a Scotty named MacTavish in *The Kennel Murder Case,* in which another dog is instrumental in identifying the killer. Robert B. Parker's Spenser has a German shorthaired pointer named Pearl. In fact, he owned a string of Pearls, along with a miniature bull terrier named Rosie. James Garner played a college cop in a movie about Dobermans trained as murderers—*They Also Kill Their Masters*. The dog is the chief suspect in a book by Clea Simon called *Dogs Don't Lie,* described as a "pet noir." Watson had a dog, unmemorably. So did Holmes in *The Hound of the Baskervilles,* but he never would have kept him as a pet. And in the story "Silver Blaze" there was the mystery of the dog that did not bark. Toby is a dog employed by Sherlock Holmes, belonging to a Mr. Sherman, introduced in *The Sign of Four* and described by Watson as an "ugly long-haired, lop-eared creature, half spaniel and half lurcher, brown and white in colour, with a very clumsy waddling gait." Holmes said he would "rather have Toby's help than that of the whole detective force in London," which, as every Baker Street Irregular knows, isn't much of a compliment.

As a boy detective, I had the family Maltese, Ami (pronouned *aah-mee*), and named for amyloidosis, a disease that attacks the heart or the spleen, on which my father was doing research. The dog died before my career in detection gained full throttle. When the kids were small, Ginny and I acquired Chloe, a frenetic cairn who was so wound up, she would race back and forth nonstop on the shelf behind the backseat of the car when we took her with us on drives. It was safer to keep her in the car than let her stay at home, where she snacked on the legs of the piano. Since Chloe was a purebred, the American Kennel Club sent a form, asking us to register her

more formal name. I filled out "Chlorox Bleachman," which
the AKC rejected. Her successor, Hector, a Westie, whom we
got for our youngest son, John, in the 1990s, had a name that
leaned toward detection, but he was more attuned to biting
the hands that fed him.

Edward Arnold played a blind detective in *Eyes in the
Night,* a clunky movie that included a Seeing Eye dog named
Friday, who possessed a large vocabulary, and could obey in-
tricate commands. "Hide behind the bed, Friday. Then open
the door and go for help." James Franciscus played a blind insurance investigator in *Longstreet,* a TV series in the 1980s,
but I cannot recall that he had a Seeing Eye dog. In fact, he
used to fight bad guys all by himself, giving a new meaning
to the idea of a handicap. Those were the days when a spate
of disabled cops and heroes appeared on TV: Tate had one
arm; Ironsides, played by Raymond Burr, rolled around in
a wheelchair. To take note of this creative nonsense, I wrote
a *Time* essay in the form of a newspaper TV schedule that
highlighted "Barker"—about a three-legged German shepherd private eye who solved crimes with his nose. The piece
was supposed to be satire. A producer phoned to ask if I'd
like to write the script.

BALANCING ON THREE paws, Ewing dragged himself toward me and licked my face. I watched him as I lay on the

couch in our oldest son Carl's house the other day. Carl named his yellow Lab after Patrick Ewing of the New York Knicks—a player I couldn't stand. But I always loved the canine Ewing, who seems able to stand anything, even on three legs. Bone cancer corrupted his left rear paw, and the limb had to go if the dog was to be saved. The vet told Carl that cancer was almost certain to show up in Ewing's lungs, and that the animal had nine more months at the outs. Ewing, ignoring his prognosis, adjusted himself in a matter of days to his tripod status, and seemed just as happy with his postoperative life as he was before. I pushed my face toward his big sloppy tongue to show him nothing had changed. Do animals say good-bye?

I don't know that I always felt as accepting of things like missing limbs as I am now, when my own old limbs aren't in such hot shape either. Legs. I, too, am on my last. It is one of the things age quietly teaches you: Everyone is disabled. Time was when I might have winced at the sight of Ewing hauling his hulking body up a flight of stairs. Now I watched, not in awe exactly, but rather in an acceptance of the way the world can change on a dime and reveal a universe of missing parts.

Four legs, two legs, three legs. I never understood why that riddle was so impenetrable to everyone but Oedipus. Any average detective could solve it. Once you eliminate all other animals and start to think metaphorically, the riddle is a cinch. More interesting, I think, is the order in which the riddle is

posed. Four, two, three, instead of counting down in reverse
order, which might have made a better riddle. The Sphinx
seems to accord a special place of honor to the crippled.

I do not mean to romanticize disabilities. No dog in his
right mind would choose three legs over four. The blind
would rather see, the deaf would rather hear. The paralyzed,
given the choice, would prefer to tango. Yet there is value in
an adjustment to the unavoidable.

At Twenty-fifth and Fifth, a beggar with eyes like rotting
grapes and a leaf stuck to his forehead rolls on a wooden platform where his legs should be, and tips over on the sidewalk.
I go to help him right himself. He does not thank me. When
he rolls away, I follow until I see him set up shop at Twenty-
fourth and Park. He stares ahead as people pass him by in the
cold. Does he remember his legs anymore, I wonder. Do they
remember him? I approach and offer him a twenty-dollar bill.
He yells he doesn't need my fucking money.

TOUGH GUY? NAH. The toughest New Yorkers I ever knew
were the residents of the Women's House of Detention, which
stood between Ninth and Tenth streets on Greenwich Avenue,
before it was demolished in 1973 and replaced by the Jefferson Market Garden. Tonight, I look up to where that prison
was, and is no more. From the rooftop exercise yard, the in-
mates called to us kids on the street below. We couldn't see

them for the fences around the exercise yard, but their voices carried out into the evenings: "Hey, Sonny. Come on up and get some." Merely the thought of getting some from a female prisoner was enough to light the night, even if most of us were hazy at best about what it meant to get some. But how free they were, lusty, brassy in captivity, their tinny voices sparking through the air like downed electric wires. They were fearless. "Come up and visit us, boys. Watcha got to lose? Your virginity?" The spinning echoes of their taunting laughter. What were the guards going to do to them? Toss them in jail?

And Tenth Street itself. In the summers, it was so crowded with trees in bloom, you could not see from one end of the block to the other. In winter, now, the sightline is clear—past the especially wide town houses, pink, white, and brown; the carriage houses; a tiny northern Italian restaurant beside an apartment house that wasn't here when I was a kid; and Holistic Pet Care. Makes me miss my holistic terriers. Tonight, I walk west on Tenth, across Greenwich Avenue toward Patchin Place, a mews of little houses, then back up the avenue, between Tenth and Eleventh, pausing at Partners & Crime, mystery-book sellers, with old copies of Dorothy Sayers, Ellery Queen, and Mickey Spillane in the window. The store must be newish. I would have remembered if it had been here before.

My first girlfriend, Abby Abrams, lived in a brownstone at the end of Tenth near Fifth. In the summer, her family invited me to their home on Fire Island. I was thirteen. Our bedrooms,

Abby's and mine, were on the second floor, across a short hall from each other. In the mornings, Abby would come into my room, wearing only a towel. A gifted artist. Big-hearted. She was a little younger than I, but way ahead of me, probably not in experience but definitely in instinct. I had no idea what was expected of me, so I just talked a blue streak. In the evenings, I'd play piano. In the daytime, I swam, swam a lot.

At the time, I did not know about the things that made Tenth Street historically noteworthy, some of which had connections to my detective work and to my life. The prison itself had a history of famous residents, including the black radical Angela Davis, the Catholic radical Dorothy Day, and Ethel Rosenberg, who awaited her execution there. A library at the corner, on Greenwich Avenue, once served as the Jefferson Market Courthouse where, in 1907, Henry K. Thaw was found insane after he'd shot and killed Stanford White, the preeminent New York architect of the period, one of whose buildings was the National Arts Club. White had been fooling around with Thaw's wife. With its salmon-color turrets and traceries, the library looks as if it had a hard time deciding not to be a castle.

Oh, but here is where George C. Scott, playing Holmes, did research in *They Might Be Giants*. And memorable real people lived on Tenth Street, too: John Reed and Louise Bryant, in number 1; E. E. Cummings, in number 4; Theodore Dreiser, Djuna Barnes, and Marlon Brando, in number 5; Mark Twain, in number 14, which was also the site of the murder of little Lisa Steinberg in the 1980s. Emma Lazarus, whose "give me your tired, your poor" poem is inscribed on the Statue of Liberty, lived in number 18. Dashiell Hammett lived in number 28, from 1947 to 1952, the height of my detective years. I wish I'd known it then.

Such information would come to me piece by piece in later life. In those days, all I knew was that at the Greenwich Avenue end of the block were the lady sirens yelling at us to come and get some, and near the Fifth Avenue end, sweet Abby was calling to me in a more innocent way to do the same thing. Someday, I hoped, I would know what all that meant. One cool thing about a private eye: He can look like he knows what he's doing, when he hasn't a clue.

Now, Ginny, I will go back with you to those evenings when we walked in Gramercy Park, made love and talked, and waited for our lives. At sixteen, each of us had evacuated our Dresden homes, in which the bomb had not detonated. It lay in our living rooms like a hog dozing, and no bomb squad would go near it. "Hair trigger," they said. "Too unpredictable." What could we do but get out of there—knowing that we would have to return to Dresden and the bomb sooner or later. But in the meantime, in the evenings, we had the shadows of trees, dark leaves, the rustle of shrubbery, the deceptive stars, the soft brown earth, and each other.

THERE WAS A women's prison of sorts in my own neighborhood, on Eighteenth between Irving Place and Third. Not a prison really, but an institution for unwed mothers who had no place else to go. Founded in 1857 by the Sisters of the Good Shepherd, the brownstone stood a few houses down from Pete's Tavern, still and neat, like a cloth coat. I paused there whenever I passed on my wanderings, occasionally catching sight of a resident coming in or out. I had only the vaguest idea of what an unwed mother meant, but it was evident that the term was both accusatory and shunning. And they were mothers, so where were their children? Those were the days, as well, when orphanages were called orphanages, all such places stating clearly and directly what they were about, though there was a little obfuscation in a home for "Friendless" women set up on Twenty-fourth Street. Official places for deserted people. The world was impelled to create a "home" for them. I wondered and noted. Sometimes I would stop in my tracks before the house on Eighteenth, and just stare at the silent door.

BETWEEN THE SECRET and the sigh. Between the laughter and the sin. Between the lies. Between the lines. Between the nights and the mornings and the pale shocked face in the glass. Between land and sea, and the silence, and the bursts of anger and the sentimental word. Between the daring and the tremor.

Between the real and the weak, and not telling them apart. Between you and me. Between you and me and the lamppost.

THE MIDDLE OF nowhere seems to me a more comforting place than the outer limits of nowhere which, logically, must be closer to somewhere. Of course, if one prefers to be somewhere, then this preference of mine must seem nuts. I can hear the Academy members right now, shouting from their tiers of wooden benches in the Academy auditorium, Sir! Who in his right mind would choose the middle of nowhere over the outer rim where, at least, one could get a glimpse of the somewhere everyone in his right mind wants to be? But, gentlemen, I would tell them, if and when I am released from the chains in which I am bound at the front of the room, beside the lectern. . . . Gentlemen, I am in my *left* mind. At which, the president of the Academy will snort, calling it the stupidest thing he has ever heard. I could not agree more, I should say, even if I understood what that meant. Or by no stretch of the imagination, for that matter.

Here in front of Gray's Papaya, at Twenty-third and Third, a boy with a face like mine, only rounder, unscarred and unlined, examines with eyes exactly like mine the people passing. Now he walks down the street amazed. I remain unmoving, like a government official, like a postal inspector, as he goes by. I see what he sees. I know what he knows. *Mon semblable.* Open as the sea. What do I feel for him? Everything. What can I do for him? Nothing. He does not notice me. He walks right through me, through my body. It's just as well. A boy like that? That boy could do anything.

"YOU MADE ME drop it!" says the string bean in the red bow tie, about six-six, who has deliberately bumped into me and deliberately dropped his BlackBerry on the sidewalk.

"The hell I did," I say. "You dropped it yourself."

"You're going to pay me for it," he says. I shake my head. "I'm gonna punch you in the face."

"Take a hike," I say, and move on.

"Fuck you!" he says, and moves on, too. What did he take me for? A rube?

ARE WE GETTING anywhere? Luckily, we're not going anywhere, so there's nowhere to get. One of the difficulties of detective work, even for an old pro, is that a false lead can divert you for years, as it does in writing, and by the time you realize you've been moving in circles, the criminal could be living high off the hog in São Paolo. But if your walk is illimitable, no trail goes cold. Such a nice scene in the movie *Body Heat,* when William Hurt, having been framed by Kathleen Turner, sits bolt upright in his prison cot as he realizes, too late, that Turner had faked her own death. She had killed the friend whose identity she had bought and assumed, tossed the body in the boathouse, incinerated it, and boom! "She's alive!" says Hurt. And all at once the scene is Brazil, with that recognizable mountain in the background, and Turner in a chaise, bored, wearing blue-lens sunglasses, and listlessly agreeing with her boy-toy Latin lover that "It's hot."

In writing, the trail goes cold all the time. The wise old prophet in whom you have placed the telling of your tale ought to have been an idiot boy, or a girl, or a dog. You started your piece of work in the inner city. You should have begun it at a lakeside resort in New Hampshire, and the whole book written in dialogue, or in rhymed couplets. And this happens in more than a single piece. Your entire existence as a writer can follow dead-end trails, and then one morning you sit bolt upright in your bed and boom! She's alive. If your desire to be a writer coincides with your desire to be noticed, why, pal, you can waste decades writing bad stuff or perfectly acceptable stuff that you simply never wanted to write. That person was you, and yet it was not. You can spend an awfully long time pursuing the cold lead of your long and winding life. Believe me. I know.

EXCEPT FOR THE CHAINS, I would not mind being a prisoner in Plato's cave. The allegory has it that the prisoners were bound and limited by more than chains because they could not see reality, and thus were deprived of the truth. They could see only the shadows of the puppets that the puppeteers cast on the cave's wall, and believed that the shadows were the puppets themselves. Being unable to turn their heads, they knew nothing of what caused the shadows. If they had seen the shadow of a book, say, or of a man, they would have mistaken appearance for reality—a destructive and unforgiveable error, according to Plato, and the theme of most of modern literature, according to university professors.

But is this so? See here: I recognize that man walking across Park Avenue South toward the Starbucks on the northwest corner of Twenty-ninth Street under the lurid light of a streetlamp. It is Sidney Homer, the man whose apartment on the ninth floor of 36 Gramercy Park mirrored our own. A Wall Street investor, he is the son of Marian Homer, the opera singer, and the grandson of Winslow Homer, the painter. When I was four or five, he used to greet me in his booming voice and ask when I planned to enroll at Harvard. When I got to Harvard eventually, the Homers gave me a leather-bound early edition of Johnson's dictionary, which I keep today in an antique book press. So there is Mr. Homer, tall and elegant, striding across the avenue to get his morning coffee. I see him clear as daylight, though he died thirty-five years ago.

Would you say that he is less real to me than the young man in the baseball cap advertising the *TODAY* show, who actually is crossing to Starbucks? The shadow of Sidney Homer is cast upon the wall of my mind's cave. "What is REAL?" the Velveteen Rabbit asks the Skin Horse, who answers that when you are loved, you begin to become real. "Does it happen all at once, like being wound up?" asks the Rabbit. "It doesn't happen all at once," said the Skin Horse. "You become. It takes a long time. That's why it doesn't happen often to people who break easily, or have sharp edges, or who have to be carefully kept." If one wants to get technical about it, the Rabbit is no more real for having been loved, or for growing old. Yet only strict Plato would say that he does not represent the truth. They say that no one ever survives old age, but that is hardly true. To the Aborigines, dreaming was the way to prolong the life about them. Here on this walk, I dwell in an eternal gloaming, just like you. We survive and love in an ageless present.

NOW THE YOUNG man sits in Starbucks, near a young woman who is reading Wallace Stevens. He says hi. She says hi. He asks where she is from. She asks if he likes snow. His arm grazes her shoulder. She comments on the traffic. He remembers the title of an old TV show. She tells him how close she is to her folks. She embraces him impulsively during a laugh. She is embarrassed, a little. He is emboldened, a little. For no reason, he thinks of Nick Nolte. For her part, she likes Nick Nolte. He wonders if she'd care to have dinner with him sometime. She says, "I'd love to have dinner with you sometime." He mentions how peaceful she seems. She looks away and says, "Thank you," and asks him something about when he was a kid. They discuss childhood, his and hers. Suddenly they both are silent, and neither says a word for quite a long while. When at last they speak, they speak at the same time, and neither can make out what the other has said. He says he is sorry about something. She says she, too, is sorry about something. But that's all right. That's all right. Now it is spring. He confesses his dreams. She makes him believe they are original and important. He begins to trust his dreams. They sit close to each other in an outdoor restaurant by the water, under a windfall of lights.

WALKING. WALKING IN Cambridge, Massachusetts. The bricks jutting out in the uneven sidewalks. The feel of brainless self-satisfaction on Brattle Street and its tributaries. Past the homes of New England aristocrats, who bred like collies, with ever-narrowing heads. Past one's fellow students who seemed stunned at recurrent news of defeat. Pointless treks. Sisyphus could be grunting beside you.

That is, unless you were walking with Professor Kelleher along the banks of the Charles, across one bridge, down the riverbank, then across another bridge. That was the way he conducted his tutorials, walking and talking. I studied Irish literature and the eighteenth-century poets with him, about which I knew nothing and cared little at first. But I cared for John Kelleher. Had he been teaching Northeastern Etruscan religious practices I would have taken that. Walks in Cambridge, and long walks in the woods near his home in Westwood, Massachusetts.

Only in appearance was he confounded by his stammer. His eyes would bulge helplessly as he would do battle with his tongue to get out a sentence. Students who did not know him fled his classes. Had they the patience to wait till his sentences were complete, they would have realized how lucky they were to be in his presence. No one ever knew more about Irish literature and history. Harvard gave him a chair while he still was in his twenties. He never went to the trouble of getting a Ph.D., because he didn't need one. And he published only one book, a slim volume of poems. He took to the eighteenth century because, like him, it had one foot in reality, the other in hope. For the nineteenth century he had little use because it confused hope with reality. Hope could go anywhere, including hell. He used to say, "Romanticism leads to Dachau."

Walking, walking, with long aggressive strides, on the riverbank and in the woods. A huge head and a severe but handsome face beneath thick white hair. Built like the boxer he had been at Dartmouth, where he'd gone by a sort of accident. He'd been repairing a roof with his father, a postman, who moonlighted as a carpenter on weekends, when one of his dad's friends stopped by to mention that he had just seen an attractive place where young John might want to go to college. When Kelleher returned from his interview, he happily reported that there were no other people there. He had seen it on spring break.

Everyone at Harvard knew something, but few knew life. Kelleher—with his hidden office in Widener Library, his amused disdain for the "fat asses in the Faculty Club," and his firm, sure strides—he knew life. He knew how to walk in the world. And so, when he taught Joyce's "Clay," he showed how it was for the old woman to be both irritating and human. And when he taught Johnson's "Vanity of Human Wishes," he could offer the world's behavior as evidence of the poem. Only once did he bother to write a scholarly article, on "The Dead." In his researches into ancient Irish history, Detective Kelleher discovered that Joyce had based the story, moment for moment, on an old Irish legend—something no one had ever pointed out, and that probably had been known to no one but Joyce himself. Then, after proving his airtight case, Kelleher ended the piece by assuring the reader that his discovery had nothing to do with enjoying the story. Ginny and I named our John after him.

ONE WALK LEADS to another. Walking in the cold mist of a Dublin late afternoon, that year we lived in Ireland. After class, while Ginny stayed at home in our rented house in the suburb of Mount Merrion, Carl growing inside her, I would walk the Dublin streets. Dark and darker. The stones of the street and the stones of the buildings shining with rain. I was twenty-four. All was ahead of us—Carl, Amy, and John, their lives, the wanderings, the jobs, Amy's death. I could have gone on forever, walking in Dublin in the late afternoons. Something about the melancholy gold of the streetlamps. Something about the woolly glow of the people. I walked in an eternal anticipation of wonders without suffering the disappointment that follows naturally. Walking between high seriousness and silliness, between ambition and weeping fits. Look at those books, like embers in the window. All of life bundled in a Dublin cold mist of a late afternoon.

And walking in the Gaeltacht, edging around the sharp rocks and the stubble hills that looked like camels' backs. I thought of J. M. Synge walking in the same place seventy years earlier, picking up the rhythms of Irish Gaelic, taking notes. At night, he sat in his attic room and listened to the rich talk he later made use of in his plays, rising through the floorboards. I picked up a little of the language sitting with my teachers in Teach Mór, Irish for "the big house," located on the Spidal Road, and taking in their stories. They didn't as much instruct as simply live, and they let you be part of their lives. They spoke English perfectly, but would not speak English to you. If you wanted anything, you had to figure out how to say it in Irish, which included going to the outhouse, which included swiping chickens, "chickini," off the seat.

But the best thing there was walking, as it always is, up and down the hills, with the wind not always at your back, and in the distance, the hard Atlantic. On the beach lay the curraghs, small black fishing boats looking like mussels on the rocks, just as they did when Synge wrote about them in *Riders to the Sea*. I would pass a farmer and greet him with "Good morning," which translated as "God to you." *"Dia duit."* And the response would add something to that. "God and Mary to you." And response to that: "God, Mary, and Joseph to you." *"Dia is Murie agus Padraic duit"*—and so on down the biblical line, till you could spend much of the morning exchanging lists of the holy personages. Or speaking of the weather, which had limited but accurate descriptions in Irish as either cold, windy, or rainy, or cold, windy, *and* rainy. Alone, you walked through the furrows, unbalanced walking, twisting your ankles, indulging mules and sheep. *"Dia is moooorie duit,"* I told a cow, who apparently had heard that one before.

AND A FEW years later, back in Cambridge, after Carl and Amy had joined us, more walking still. Walks were all the entertainment we could afford. So, when we were living in Dunster House, we took walks along Memorial Drive, strollers and clanking fire engines banged around by the winds off the river. And when we were living on Bowden Street, walks on Mass Ave., north as far as Sears, and back home. There was a shop where a little man made violins. And a church with a sign, kind of an ad, behind glass: THIS ENDS YOUR SEARCH FOR A FRIENDLY CHURCH. Garden Market, run by a nice guy named Doc, where we got our food. The drugstore where I was careful to buy only the five-pack of razor blades, and the cleaners where we were careful only to have things pressed. The window of an antiques shop displayed a small round wood table I liked. The tag said $7. I thought: We can afford that. The saleswoman tried not to sound condescending. "That means seven hundred," she said.

On a walk in a different part of Cambridge, Ginny and I passed a shop selling the Eames Chair, new then, with-it, sharp and hopeful, we thought, just as we wanted to be. It too cost $700, but I asked the store owner if I might pay it off in monthly installments, and he said sure. We had no paintings to cover our apartment walls, so I bought some prestretched canvases, and painted them myself. Amateurish geometrical designs, which no one found revolting. From an exposed beam in our apartment we hung the Jolly Jumper, a little seat on elastic cords, on which Amy bounced, endlessly smiling. She loved it. She loved her Marx motorcycle—she and Carl racing on the sidewalks, Ginny and I apologizing to the scattering pedestrians.

IN THE SAME way that a magician summons a crystal ball into the air, from a table with a cloth on it—into the air where, mirabile dictu, it hovers suspended, trembling—in the same way as that, I call forth your face, like a light balloon, before my eyes. (How does he *do* that?) Where do you walk now, my sweet girl?

DEATH IS A little thing. I do not mean that it lacks significance or pain. Only that it happens. And that's that. You live with the living and you live with the dead. Here today, gone later today, like the Tutsis in Rwanda, another case I worked on, who were walking with their kids one moment and chopped to death the next. Slack at the top of the waterfall over the Kagera River, the bodies rose and fell. One, two, fifty. I watched them from where I stood on a bridge—the bright yellow bridge that was not there one day, and one day it was, so that the people of Tanzania could walk to Rwanda, and the people of Rwanda could walk to Tanzania, with baskets of fruit on their heads, and kids at their sides.

You can never tell where your feet will lead you. Genesis has it that God took a walk one evening and came upon Adam, who was naked and hiding, thus revealing to God that he had eaten from the tree. The first recorded walk. Makes you wonder whether Adam and Eve would still be in Eden transgressing their tails off if God had not felt like taking an evening stroll. One thing for certain: Eden would have been a hell of a lot more interesting.

What did I start to say to you? Do you recall? At least
you'll remember the nights when the swells of the sea lapped
at the screen door. Is that what I started to say? Mountains
were involved, I'm pretty certain. And wheat bundled in rolls
in a gray field. A giant green Coke bottle embossed on the
side of a warehouse. And a warehouse that dissolved into ce-
dars in Vermont. And a water leak that seeped into the walls
and made hieroglyphic stains. The transitional light of evening. The tributes at an awards dinner around the table covered with white linen. A herd of boozing sheep. They played
a role, too, I think. I can't be sure.

WHERE THINGS ARE, where they were. I approach the
New York Public Library at Forty-second and Fifth. In high
school I used to track down mystery books here, combing
the vast marble halls for books and more books, order-
ing them, and stunned when they magically appeared, just
like that. Request a book, get a book. The library opened
in 1911, on the site that once held the Croton Distributing
Reservoir, built in 1842, to meet the city's need for fresh
water. Fed by the Croton Reservoir north of the city, by way
of forty miles of pipes, the Distributing Reservoir was a four-
mile, manmade lake, contained by walls fifty feet high and
twenty-five feet thick. Citizens strolled the promenade along
the top, taking in views of Manhattan. Poe wrote of taking

walks there. Water was borne through underground pipes, moving through the thirsty city as books did later. Where things are, where they were. In *Go Tell It on the Mountain,* James Baldwin's boy detective, John Grimes, beholds the Public Library from the base of the steps on which the two great stone lions perch. The black boy wonders if the lions are there to protect him once inside the library, or to keep him out.

Forty-second Street. Thirty-eighth Street. Fourteenth. Twenty-second. First Avenue. Second. Third. Avenues A, B, and C. The grid of the city, laid out in 1811 and stretching from Houston Street downtown to 155th Street in Harlem, makes it easy to find where you are going. The numbers are consecutive. East and west divide at Fifth. Plain as the nose on your face. But what lies beneath this neat construction? To learn that takes detective work. The streets have their order, but the houses on them all are different. A deli lit too brightly. A cigar store looking like a crushed hat. And underneath all this? Crocodiles swim in the sewers, so they say. Bloodstained bricks in the walls of deserted tunnels. Dungeons and dragons.

The city planners made the grids deliberately, I think—to give the impression of control on the surface, the way a face controls itself, smiles brightly, and greets the day. But see the confusion and the desperation below. The lower depths, full of broken china and live cables. Screams and anarchy. Twentieth Street. Twenty-first Street. Dig there.

YET HERE'S HOW memory can let you down, students: The back of 36 Gramercy, the side opposite the park, faces a courtyard roughly twenty-five feet deep and eighty feet wide. We used to ride bikes there, and play baseball. Over the years, I smashed more than one window in number 34, the back of which also faced the courtyard and served as center field. One or another of us kids would hit a shot, glass would crash and fly, and we were bats out of hell.

It was, in fact, a hellish place, the courtyard. Unlike the white terra-cotta facade of 36, the other side of the building was composed of bricks blackened by soot. If the front of the building was shimmering upper-middle-class New York, the rear was the gloom of the city, a tenement built into a wall. And in that wall was a small tunnel, no more than four feet high and six feet long, which led to an airshaft that shot up the full height of the building. You would bend low and move carefully through the tight confines of the lightless tunnel and emerge into the tarnished silver light of the sky cast into the airshaft.

We named our tunnel the Peanut Gallery, after the kids' section of the live audience of the *Howdy Doody Show*. But our Peanut Gallery had no laughter of delight. It was a place where forbidden things happened. Exchanges of contraband, toy guns, were transacted there. And bullying. And the lighting of Chinese firecrackers. Photos of naked women were given scrupulous examination. In the Peanut Gallery, girls showed you theirs if you showed them yours.

All well and good, or not so good, but here's the thing, as Detective Monk is wont to say: At any time of my life, had you asked me where the Peanut Gallery was, I would have told you unhesitatingly that it was located to the left of the back door of 36. To the left, without a doubt, about twenty feet in. A few years ago, I happened to be in the old neighborhood, and I was moved to walk through the gilded lobby of the building, straight to the back and out the door, into the courtyard. I looked to my left, and saw only the wall. I looked to my right, and there the entrance to the Peanut Gallery yawned like a black cave. To my right. Now, tell me why, all these years, did I get it wrong. Was I so afraid or ashamed of the sinful hole that my mind hid it from itself? Or was I thinking of another place entirely, even darker and more dreadful, that I had obliterated into forgetfulness?

Sometimes I wondered, whenever I crawled through that dark place alone, what would happen if the roof of the little tunnel collapsed and I was imprisoned in the airshaft and buried in the ruins. Did I have the strength and skill to shimmy up the drainpipe that ran along the side of the shaft to the roof of the building? Could I climb twelve stories, and then stand on the roof and look down upon the world of crimes?

WE GET THIS every so often: a disaster story about the collapse of a coal mine in Wales or Kentucky, men trapped in the shaft. Or people caught under the rubble after an earthquake, or a tornado or an avalanche. No sound emits from the survivors. And then there comes what the newspeople call a "miracle." Someone stuck beneath the piles of rocks or the debris of a house makes a little signal to announce "I'm alive!" And the earthmovers go into action, and the forklifts. And the rescue workers paw frantically at the floorboards and at the boulders to get to the source of the sound. "It was pure luck that I happened to hear it," they say. The clink of a spoon against a wall, the sound so faint it is hard to know what inspires it. Could be desperation. Could be impatience. A tapping from the ruins.

The thing about ruins is that they are enjoyed both for what they are and for what they were. The former engages an appreciation of the present, the latter of an imagined past. The evidence of both lies in chipped noses and decayed arms and legs, pillars sprawled like white logs in a cleared wood. We can picture the stages of disintegration of the Roman theater, or of Nineveh or Babylon, each place once a confident paradise before it fell gradually into sand and dust. Columns standing without the roofs of temples. Gods with human heads. The claws of beasts, winged lions, bulls, blank-staring kings in Syria, South America, Cambodia. The world in ruins, each pile a monument to art and power. Greek cities taken by Croesus, then Cyrus, then Darius, glorified by Ptolemies, destroyed by Seleucids, swallowed up by Rome, ravaged by Turks, and then the Crusaders, and then the Turks again.

Everyone buries someone or something. Evidence lies in bones. Ricardo Montalban starred in *Mystery Street* as a dogged policeman who partners with a forensic expert. They begin with the discovery of a woman's skeleton, no clues as to her identity, and end catching the blackguard who killed her. The movie was based on a true case, in a small town in Massachusetts. The waste remains, as William Empson says in "Missing Dates." And what is left is as significant as what originally was intact. Rome. Nineveh. Babylon. The gaping holes, like mouths. The places where walls were. All the plundered haunts, a shrine to lizards and a plaza for owls.

Give thanks for the owls. Give thanks for the ghosts. For the paper and the clay jars. For the golden stripes of the sun. Give thanks for the pain. For the faint music playing in the stranger's house. I pass by it now, on Fifteenth Street between First and Second, with the deep purple curtains drawn like a mood and the heavy black door with the brass knocker and the chipped paint. Give thanks for the chipped paint, and for all that is broken and missing. For the dark geometry of the streets, and the ornamental streetlamps, and the dead trees. And for the ruins. By all means, for the ruins.

SPEAKING OF MEMORY—were we speaking of memory?— you may be wondering if I invented the Norwegians. Me, too. I refer to that summer when I was six in Weston, Connecticut.

On one of my bike excursions one morning, I came upon a family from Norway, sitting on a lawn. A mother with a smiling face. A father with jet-black hair and a jaw like a plow. A son, a few years older than I, named Arvid. All three were very nice to me. The parents were about to send a birthday card to their daughter back in Norway. "How do you say 'happy birthday' in your language?" I asked them. *"Yertlig Helslinger,"* they said, and they proceeded to compose their note, which read, *"Yertlig Helslinger, de mama, papa, uck Arvid."*

For some sixty years, I held that phrase in my head—*"Yertlig Helslinger"*—hoping that someone would ask me how to say "happy birthday" in Norwegian or, even better, that I might meet a Norwegian on his or her birthday. It's just as well that neither occasion presented itself, because recently, having learned at last to Google, I decided to confirm my memory of the phrase. In case you're interested, pal, it turns out that "happy birthday" in Norwegian is *"Gratulerer med dagen."* From this, one may reasonably conclude that I invented the Norwegians. Who knows? In any case, I wish you and yours a very *Yertlig Helslinger.*

I FEEL MORE assured offering you two rules from what is called the Golden Age of detective fiction (1920–1939). The first is that the private eye cannot know anything the reader does not know. He cannot cheat or manipulate the reader

by coming up with an ending that depends on information
we did not have all along. Even in the inverted-plot stories
where we are shown the criminal and the crime at the outset, as in Graham Greene's *Brighton Rock* or in the *Columbo*
TV series, where we watch the detective piece everything together so that he arrives at the place known to us from the
start—even then, the detective cannot learn what we have not
already learned. It must be proven that we were able to antici-
pate the ending, even if we were unaware that we could do it.
The second rule (sorry) is that the detective cannot commit
the crime. Keep that in mind as we move along.

THUMBS-UP FOR THAT one there, who inspects his reflection in the window of Glatt's Kosher on Thirteenth Street off
First. Yes, that one. If his presentation goes well this morning, I mean really well, with no glitches like last week, when
he dropped the box of pencils, and made forced jokes about
dropping the ball; if he didn't drop the ball this time, and everyone, and I mean everyone, including Charles himself, gave
him the thumbs-up; if he wasn't all thumbs this time, and the
account, THE ACCOUNT, was his; and then he could run to
his cubicle and tweet Sarah, who looked so much like Naomi
Watts you would swear she *was* Naomi Watts, but who has
been looking elsewhere lately, maybe more bored than elsewhere, but in any case, clearly (inasmuch as anything between

two people can be clear) wants to drop him like a box of pencils and go back to her bar-hopping days, when she would allow herself to be picked up by the nearest douche bag in a grin, suit, and tie; if he could tell her about THE ACCOUNT and the thumbs, so that she could see that he would amount to something, after all—which his mother, Grace, always said about him, even if his dad, Warren, said he didn't have a Chinaman's chance, which coincidentally was what his Chinese professor at Bucknell (Was that the best school you could get into? Sarah had asked on their second date at Olive Garden), had told him, at least as far as learning Chinese was concerned, though the Bucknell Chinese professor did not say he didn't have the chance of a Caucasian, ha-ha—I mean, if that is the issue, and not the fact that at age thirty-two, he cannot get it up for more than two minutes at a time, which condition makes him so nervous that he wonders about the difference between Cialis and Viagra, and droops like a wet pennant long before climbing into bed with Sarah, who by this time could not care less, and in fact he is getting it up right now as he inspects his reflection in the window of Glatt's Kosher, experiencing the first real hard-on he's had in months, brought on by the anticipation of a successful presentation this morning, not to mention THE ACCOUNT, after which Charles will give him the thumbs-up; and see? He's got it up at last, everything up—well then, if that all happens, well then, everything, and I mean everything is going to be, in PI lingo, jake.

IN CONTRAST, PLEASE turn your attention to cool dude who sits at the wheel of his Escalade, texting. He is stopped at a light now. But he will be texting later as well, on the FDR Drive, where he is heading at Twentieth Street and the river, during which texting he will die, taking a few others with him. His text will begin, BTW, WHERE R U? OMG . . ." and proceed no further. For the moment, though, he is safe at the light. Approaching that corner on foot is a young man of business, in a light gray suit and no topcoat. Another cool dude. His stride is cool. As is that of the girls in the red satin jackets of their high school volleyball team. The jackets are cool as well. The cop directing traffic also looks cool in his dark blue uniform, hard as a frozen roast. He notices me. I would try to look cool myself, but I am not cool.

I think too weirdly to be cool. To wit: What if I were to toss a stone into the middle of this pond? Would the ripples touch the cop and the volleyball team, and then, widening, would they touch the young man of business? And finally, would the ripples reach the man texting in his Escalade? Before, I mean. Before he steps on the gas, and dies, taking a few others with him.

LET ME TAKE that back, what I said earlier about dreams, or partly back. Wordsworth wrote, "Our birth is but a sleep and a forgetting." Hard to tell what the poet wishes us—to awaken into a dream state and call it life? Sha-boom? Well, I'll give him this: life does feel like a dream much of the time. But that's a long way from actually being one. And the safe distance from events that you can manufacture, or will, in a dream, that doesn't happen when you're awake. Life does not create protections from itself. There is a reality, you know. And, *pace,* Bill Wordsworth, it does not exist in the before-life. How hopeful they were, those Romantic boys. Coleridge snatching a baby out of its pram, to the horror of the child's mother, and beseeching it to "Tell me about heaven!" Still, the idea has legs—"heaven lies about us in our infancy." Sha-boom.

What it depends on is our intuition of an immortal existence, Frankenstein minus the panic—a remembrance of things past, which things are only pure and joyful. If nothing else, such intimations suggest that we are better creatures than we appear, nobler than the ones who act in our name. I do love these poets. Yet, I cannot help but wonder what terrible sadness drove them to see the life about them as not really happening. With sadness as the impetus, the yearning for dreams makes sense. Then, immortal intimations may be seen not as philosophy, but rather as a consolation for living in a world that is sometimes harsh and often pitiless. You are standing beside the one you love, on a gray glacier, in the airless center of the moon, just after reality has clobbered you. Sha-boom. What would you say? Life is but a dream, sweetheart?

BEFORE THE DREAM turned into a state of enlightenment, I shone my industrial-strength flashlight into the last dark closet on the right, and was inclined to remain. But, as it always does, the waking world insisted on itself, and I sat up in bed. Call that reality? Nero was reality. He had a statue of himself erected in one of his several palaces. One hundred and fifty feet high. When it was done, he gazed upon it and said, "At last I am beginning to live like a human being."

CAUGHT IN THE tangled yarn of the wind, the rich old dear plows on like the Russian army. I track his every step. He is loveless, without love. He holds himself to blame, yet wonders how it is that his life has come to this. Will love ever watch over him again? For no reason he can come up with, he thinks the lyrics of "I've Been Working on the Railroad," following the entire song through its wandering narrative. Near the end, his partner Max, though a skeptic in all things, took up spiritualism and astrology, and announced that he'd be back. It has been sixteen years without a signal. Without a word. Just like Max. Are the servants in tonight? he asks himself, as he approaches his gingerbread apartment house on Thirty-third and Park. He surveys the landscape of his building and sees a light in a window like unpolished silverware. Someone's in the kitchen with Dinah.

SOME FULL OF VINEGAR. Some full of sorrow. Some quick to anger. Some slow to burn. Some apologize. Some never apologize and walk with a stutter step. Some speak Spanish. Some do not. Some forget to mail a love letter that took three weeks to compose, and, to date, has taken three weeks to mail. Some are precancerous. Some are postmodern. Some consider the many. Some consider only themselves and are, nonetheless, quite charming, and make a good first impression. Some recall Achilles, and some never heard of Achilles, who, for his part, never heard of them.

Sail on, my fellow voyagers. Sail under a clear sky, in the rolling forest of the night. Sail, and be safe. And, to be sure, I take note of your tentative movements. But see, even the snow hesitates tonight. We all sail with the same fear in the wind. From a great quiet you came, and toward a great quiet you proceed. Look there, in the black sky, on the port side of the horizon, a bright badge spewed with spices. Lo! Hark! The singing and chatter of life! And remember what Thetis told Achilles, that he had not long to live. And when the frightened Achilles reported to Patroclus what she had said, Patroclus told him: Pay no attention to her. She's a god. She tells that to everyone.

Long live the red dust on the stoops. Long live the ankle-length garment of the false prophet who skitters across the ramp at Fortieth and Park. Long live the weeds that insist upon voicing their opinions from the crevices of the chipped asphalt. Long live the obscenity. Long live the walk.

You can't go for a successful walk in an agitated or fretful state of mind. Try it, and your pace will quicken to a near trot, or slow to a near crawl, a snail's pace. The true walk requires a mind finely balanced between confidence and excitement. And if you are not of such a mind when you start out, the walk itself sometimes will create it in you. But you must be open to change. Like detective work, good walking is for liberals. Your correct state of mind is neither passionate nor dispassionate. It is a smile without the mouth turned up. It takes in and gives out as well, being at once idle and hard at work. Such a balanced stance suits the flaneur, the literary wanderer who creates the sights he takes in. Wordsworth was a flaneur of the countryside, as De Quincey was a flaneur of the city. Whitman was known as a "boulevardier," an elegant stroller. Frank O'Hara made mental maps as he walked in New York. His world grew lovelier, ecstatic.

I wonder what my personal cartographer would make of my territory. Haphazard map, lurching its way through the crazy syntax of side streets and three random parks, then up the avenues that changed their names, and east to the river with a million currents, and west to the middle of Manhattan, if you please. Cut out all the surrounding acreage, and what have we? *Hic sunt dracones.* My compass spins out of whack. My legend unreadable, my navigations berserk. In the deepest frost, snow falling like ashes, my cartographer goes about with pencil and sextant. Is this the New World? I ask him. Always has been, he says.

Winter. Winter. A cerement in the word. Two homeless men and one homeless woman pile themselves together on the steps of the Marble Collegiate Church at Twenty-ninth and Fifth. The men have hair like thatched roofs. The woman is a cartridge shell. They stare at me like rifles. Their canteens are empty, their gear spread wide like flattery. I want to ask them how the battle went, much less the war. The woman mutters, "Gawd." Where is Matthew Brady when you need him?

WHERE'S JOHNNY MORRIS when you need him, I'd like to know, when America has no natural heroes left and every so-called national leader looks twice before he fails to leap. Not Johnny Morris. He who organized evening tackle football games in the park (I used Peter's diapers as shoulder pads). He who printed programs for the games, and positioned flashlights in the trees to illuminate the gravel field, and saw to it that all the neighborhood parents were invited. He who protected the little guy, especially his younger brother, Mark. He included everyone. He who established snow forts and capture-the-flag games and ring-a-levio, and who said one fine spring day,

"You be the pitcher." So I became a pitcher. He who got a Nok Hockey game for Christmas, and when I told my dad that I wanted one, too, Johnny said, "You don't need a game of your own. If I have one, we all have one." He who papered the wall of his room at number 34 with full-page photos of pro athletes, ripped out of *Sport* magazine. And when he did that, so did I. When his dad suddenly switched jobs, the Morrises moved up to Westchester and the air went out of Gramercy Park, and the light and the shout. Whenever Johnny carried the football tucked to his chest, he half-sang, half-muttered "They Always Call Me Mr. Touchdown" under his breath, as an accompaniment to his game. He used to say I was the smart one.

IN PENNSYLVANIA, on an overnight at summer camp, a bunch of us boys strayed from the group and went for an evening walk, on which we came upon a deserted farmhouse. One lame-brained kid, who used to amuse himself by pulling the legs off frogs, casually tossed a rock at an upstairs window. He missed. Another boy came closer, his rock hitting just below the sill with a slap. Then all the boys picked up rocks and hurled them at the empty gray farmhouse. Its paint was peeling. It stood like a headstone against the slate of the sky. A few minutes passed. I watched the others throw their rocks, and considered whether or not I wanted to join in. Then, acting on a reflex more than a thought, I picked up an especially good rock and threw it at that upstairs window. I was a pitcher. I did not miss.

Drink in the fresh-mowed grass. Grind the dirt under your cleats. Stare in. Turn away. Do we ever leave our childhood? "Roger is a good athlete" read my second-grade report card. "But he doesn't like to play with other children." More problem than compliment in that, since most of the sports one plays require the cooperation of other children. Consider the person who can play with his peers but chooses not to, and so is left in a self-confounding position—he who stands alone among other players, elevated, the center of attention who is at the same time ignored by his teammates, expendable and indispensable, at once in and out of the game.

The thing about pitching, about being a pitcher, is that you want to make the batter appreciate what you have thrown at him, but only after the ball has settled in the catcher's mitt. The batter looks at the ball, and then at you. You look at him, but only briefly, a glance. You don't want to taunt him. You let the ball do that. And then he looks away, as in a dream, having coming to terms with the fact that the only way to understand what you have done is when it is too late for him to do anything about it. Like detective work. Like writing.

MY FATHER, game to play catcher, crouches for me in the driveway of an inn we are staying at in Southampton. I pitch to him, too fast, maybe. Unthinkingly, maybe. A rare flicker of fear in his eyes as he reaches for the ball—the flicker I saw years later, after his first heart attack. Then it was submerged. Now it lies on the surface, and is laced with his being impressed with me—rarer still—impressed that I can throw as fast as that. In fact, my fastball seemed fast only to him. In my first varsity game in high school, my first pitch, a fastball, hit the batter in the shoulder. I stepped off the mound to see if he was okay. He stood at the plate, chuckling.

A game of catch between father and son. A game of catch between me and our children. Not quite the same as pitcher-catcher, which is more purposeful, more aggressive, but generally the same idea. The ball flies between the generations, between the hearts and minds. It's not called "throw," that game, because the idea is that you'll catch each other, that father and children will understand each other in the silent way we do. My father and I understand each other, in the driveway.

Richard Wilbur visited a modern poetry class I was teaching at Harvard in the 1960s. He listened to my students interpret several of his poems, then said, to their delight: "It's nice to meet people who catch what you're throwing." Especially a curve.

WRITING IS unreasonably demanding. A tyrant, a regular Stalin, when you get down to it. Why do I have to produce an ocean in the morning, much less paint the sun-streaks on it, much less the plaster clouds or the goddam sun itself? What do you take me for, anyway—a court magician, a wizard in a stupid star-splashed dunce's hat? A down-and-out sketch artist on lower Fifth on a Sunday afternoon, awaiting your ten bucks so that I might make your chin more manly or give you a nose job in charcoal? I'm not God, for Chrissake, or Christ, for God's sake. I'm not your father, either, if that's what you're thinking, and even if I were your father, aren't you old enough by now to fetch your own ocean? Oh, never mind. I'm just venting. You didn't create this case. I did. I, and the smirking sheet of paper that says, in the greasy voice of a racetrack tout, how about an ocean this morning, pal? Yeah. And make it original.

NATURALLY, YOU DON'T get there all at once, or on your own. It took two seasoned private eyes to show me the ropes. The first was Rowse B. Wilcox, whom I had only for ninth grade English, but that was enough to begin forging the connection between literature and detective work. He was too drunk too often, so the school canned him. To be sure, he had been indispensible to hundreds of students for decades, but he was dying anyway. Why not send him into exile? So Mr. Wilcox took up his final residence here where I am now, at the Prince George Hotel on Twenty-eighth Street between Madison and Fifth, built in 1904 and restored to much of its former grandeur after decades as a flophouse. Our first real teacher, he taught us that a verb could contain the force of a noun, as in "the leaf pinwheeled to the ground." He taught us the difference between drama and melodrama. "Drama is opposed activity with conflict. Melodrama is opposed activity without conflict." Bony, like Lincoln, he sat up in front of the room at the chipped wooden desk, legs crossed like chopsticks. He had a lusty reputation with the girls. I do not remember his voice.

When, in my sophomore year, I heard that he was living out his days at the Prince George Hotel, I went to visit him. He greeted me in the lobby, and we chatted among the faux antiques and the Victorian bric-a-brac in one of the public rooms, sitting in plush purple armchairs with tears in the upholstery. Pastel columns held up the room, in which there also was a dry fountain, faded murals, and a fire going under a cracked marble mantelpiece. A tall mirror rose above the mantelpiece and a crystal chandelier, disproportionately large, above that. He wore a tie and a suit jacket that did not match his pants. The jacket was gray, the pants brown. His vest hung loose. His eyes were bleary, but he had shaved. His shirt cuffs were stained with tobacco. He was pleased to see me, I believe. Perhaps he was pleased to have any visitors at all.

Walking home, I remember feeling sad and helpless, and that I was losing someone who held the secrets of the life I dimly sought, someone I might trust. A grown-up I might trust. We did not talk long. Half an hour, maybe a little more. He chain-smoked and said interesting things that I forget. He did most of the talking, since I had little to say but thank you.

SEE WHAT YOU make of this dream, in which I decided to spend the night at the Prince George Hotel myself. When I registered at the desk, I learned from the clerk, who was the spitting image of Elisha Cook Jr. as he appeared in *The Maltese Falcon,* that Dylan Thomas was staying in the hotel, was in fact living there, since Caitlin had thrown him out for good this time. He had lurched at too many breasts, two too many. No, wait. It wasn't Dylan Thomas. It was Tennessee Williams, that's who was there, just for the night. But since I favored poets in those days, I'm saying it was Dylan Thomas staying in the hotel. And when I gathered the courage to introduce myself to him that evening, in the bar, over a grasshopper, I told him I was Tennessee Williams, just to put myself on an even footing with him, and I extended my hand. But, he said, politely but firmly, as southern gentlemen do, "*I* am Tennessee Williams." "Are you certain?" I asked. He nodded, smiling. So then I said, feeling bolder by the second, that that must mean *I* am Dylan Thomas. And before he could recover his composure, because he was meeting Dylan Thomas at last, whom he had admired all those years, while never stooping to say, "I'm a big fan," I retreated to my room in the hotel, the little red one that shared a bath with Samuel Beckett, who, as luck would have it, was also an overnight guest. And I spent the entire night sleepless, though ecstatic, considering a rapprochement with Caitlin, while writing "The Hunchback in the Park."

CRIPPLES, DRUNKS, LECHERS, madmen. Is it possible to sympathize with everyone? That is what we are supposed to do on our illimitable walk, or so they say. How about Pol Pot or the Japanese soldiers in Nanking or our own soldiers at My Lai? Joyce's Bloom sympathized with everyone, and see where it got him. I don't know. I like Joyce's bourgeois Ulysses and Robert Graves's girl-crazy Ulysses well enough, I suppose, but I much prefer the original wild sailor, or even Tennyson's old salt who strove, sought, found, and did not yield.

It is assumed of such heroes, people of certain magnitude, as Aristotle put it and Matthew Arnold repeated, that they are above sympathizing with the lower orders. But there is no evidence of that, one way or the other. What drove Quixote to attack the giants? What drove George C. Scott's Sherlock Holmes, in all the nuttiness of his quest for Moriarty, but the desire to ennoble the world for everyone, not just for himself? This is the detective's kind of sympathy. And the writer's. Both see people for what they are,

judging privately, yet leaving cosmic judgment to others—
perhaps the deepest sort of sympathy there is.

And love gets in the act. It does. The detective may seek
honor over love, yet ideally he wants both. Love personal and
love general. For all his hard-boiled patter, he believes that
love defines us, that if love prevailed over all competing emo-
tions in the first place, there would be no cupidity, no crime.
He knows we are composed of the choices we make, sometimes imprisoned by them. Yet he also knows, though he does
not say so, that love trumps all our choices. If memory acknowledged nothing but love, we would be so light-hearted,
we would be able to fly. But we are not able to fly. Even the
dumbest PI knows that. The dumbest and the saddest.

Of course, sympathy does not imply trust. Detectives find
it best not to trust anyone. It's encumbering, I know, living
with mistrust as a constant, but that is how it must be in order
to solve a mystery and bring about justice. And it works both
ways, after all. I don't trust you yet, pal. You don't trust me.

And all this wariness extends to a mistrust of human nature as well. So sad. I cannot tell you how many cases I've
been on where someone protests, "Him? He couldn't have
done it. He doesn't have it in him." Alas, he had it in him.
Everyone has it in him. And before you point out that there's a
logical contradiction between seeking to save people and not
believing they are worth saving, allow me to point out that it is
not other people the detective is saving. Most of the time, the

detective strives to save himself, whom he also doesn't trust. It's true. Trust me.

I sound as though I read a lot as a boy, but, except for detective fiction, I didn't. More bookstoreish than bookish, I often took my pursuits to the Fourth Avenue bookstores between Ninth and Fourteenth streets. Caves on a boulevard, where the antique books, like shelves of rocks, extended deep into mists. If there had been any order to the inventory, it was buried in the minds of the proprietors, old Commies mainly, who rarely looked up from whatever manifesto they were reading. Each one sat monklike in the front of his shop, by the door, and raised an eyelid or two as you entered. A kid, even a detective, would receive no notice. It hardly mattered. My business was not with the old men, but rather with the books—black, brown, maroon. The sweet-dust smell. The dates of old publications. I bought a biography of Napoleon written in the 1880s, and the essays of Macaulay, and short stories by Jack London. Everything dirt cheap.

I can't remember ever reading any of them. What I sought from the books was a connection to past mysteries. In the best detective stories, something terrible that happened long ago erupts in a crime of the present. I would nose around one store after another (there were at least twenty-five of them), as if I were hunting for something specific. The proprietors never questioned my motives. They understood what I wanted. It was the same thing they had wanted when they had relocated their lives to a bookstore. Quiet, strange, dark. No money in it for them. Eventually they moved to Florida.

Two bookstores are left in the area these days. The Alabastar, between Eleventh and Twelfth streets, is not one of the originals, as it was established in 1996. But it has the look and feel of the great old stores. The Strand, founded in 1927, has hung on all these years, among the newer enterprises of art supply centers, low-rise apartments, and stores that sell Halloween costumes and "fantasy apparel." Everything looks alike, but so did the old bookstores. They just looked better, alike. A friend of John's works in the Strand. He reports whenever a book of mine winds up in the one-dollar bin. "Overpriced," he says. I go to the Strand from time to time, but today it's a little too café and eager to please for my taste. I think it feels abandoned. I think it misses the companionship of the other stores. I try to picture the day they went out of business. A truck pulls up out front. The books are carried out like patients from a nursing home. And for a moment, before demolition, the obvious vacant walls.

NOTHING MUCH AT Twenty-fourth and Fifth, though once there was a great arch here. Erected in 1918, it was bigger than the one that stands today at the end of Fifth Avenue in

Washington Square Park. That arch was built in 1889, to honor the centennial of George Washington's first inauguration. The arch on Twenty-fourth was built to honor the soldiers of the city who had died in the First World War. Mayor Fiorello LaGuardia denounced the structure as the "altar of extravagance," and the arch was razed shortly after a victory parade in 1918. What remains is a fifty-one-foot-high obelisk called the Worth Monument, after General William Jenkins Worth, who fought in the Mexican-American War. War dominates the city's monuments, every city's probably. Yet the monuments evoke no sense of power or glory. Stone generals on stone horses overlook the citizens, who pay no attention to them. A comedian of my childhood years said that he hoped to erect a statue of a pigeon, so that all the generals for miles around could sit on it.

In a despotic government, the hero is the man who robs a train. But that does not excuse him for relishing his life of crime. Enjoyment of that sort creates a tyranny of its own. I do not know what makes a hero. Something hidden and unnoted, probably, such as you dressing in the morning, and preparing to meet the world, my hero.

IN *THE WALK,* Jeffrey C. Robinson calls walking a "quintessentially Romantic image" because it is associated with happiness. Not that Romanticism was always all that happy, but I see his point. The walks or marches for civil rights had a goal of happiness before them in the betterment of lives. Walks in the nineteenth century were meant to offer a leisurely opposition to the dark satanic mills of the Industrial Revolution. There are religious pilgrimages undertaken with the hope of a sort of happiness. The idea of progress is also associated with walks, by seeking to go one step further. Gulley Jimson, the loony painter of Joyce Cary's *The Horse's Mouth,* had as his life's ambition the creation of a gigantic wall depicting human feet, indicating that the part of us we walk on is the noblest part.

Am I taking this walk to find happiness? I did not think so at first. I thought I was simply dwelling in a mystery. Yet meandering like this, sans pressure, feels akin to happiness. So yes, it is possible that I have undertaken this walk of mine to feel better about myself, about everything. If I walk from the present into the past, as I have been doing, I may even feel better about the past. Happiness in the past. Is that possible?

"Do you know," said my mother, "that you sang 'Daisy, Daisy' while you were still in the carriage?"

"I did?"

"And in your crib. You stood up, hanging on to the wooden railing, and sang, 'Daisy, Daisy, give me your answer true.'"

" 'Give me your answer true,' " I repeated.

She continued to sing. " 'I'm half crazy . . .' "

And I: " ' . . . all for the love of you.' "

WHAT'S ALL THIS about not stepping on a shadow? What exactly are you afraid of? That the shadows will feel your hobnail boot on them and cry out in pain? That they will suck you into the pavement like quicksand, your arms flailing, beseeching, as you go under, hands reaching out from the grave? Why, there were kids in our neighborhood who would sooner step on a crack and break their mothers' back, before they ever would step on a shadow. If they spotted a shadow ahead of them, especially at night when shadows are hard to spot, they would rev up like racing cars in order to leap over the terrible blot. One boy I knew, who lived on Eighteenth and Third, name of Daley, was so afraid of shadows he'd turn back if he saw one, returning to where he came from, or travel all the way round Robin Hood's barn rather than confront the dark ghost on the street. Not me. I was hardly brave, but fear a shadow? Never. Shadows are too potent. They contain one's inner value. A private eye would no more avoid a shadow than a pilot would the sky. One time, I took a picture of my shadow under a traffic light, so that it appeared like a person with a traffic light for a head. Why I did this I have no clue. But it goes to show how comfortable I felt with shadows, that I would become one. Besides, using a traffic light that way made it easier to direct the stories I made up, or did not make up.

STOP HERE: the Jewish cemetery on Eleventh Street between Fifth and the Avenue of the Americas. A sign denotes the Second Cemetery of the Spanish and Portuguese synagogue congregation, Shereath Israel (1805–1829). The First Cemetery of the Spanish and Portuguese synagogue congregation, on Chatham Square in Chinatown, dates back to the 1640s and contains soldiers who fought in Washington's army. There is yet a Third, on Twenty-first Street. But this is the one I kept returning to as a kid. Just standing and peering in at the haphazard triangle, the unkempt garden tucked between buildings.

Maybe thirty-five, thirty-six graves here, with three scrawny trees and a sapling standing among the headstones. Only one substantial monument, consisting of a square stone base beneath a chunky obelisk. Two flat stone markers. One crypt the size of a largish hope chest. The other graves are marked by whitish stones leaning against the cemetery's back wall, like wallflowers at a dance. Some are small, suggesting the graves of children. One has the shape of a cartoon ghost, sculpted by rain and erosion. All the inscriptions are worn away. Mute inglorious Miltons. Does anyone read Thomas Gray these days?

Charles Ives occupied the town house next to the cemetery. I don't know what he made of it. As a boy, I don't know what I made of it either, except to acknowledge how unusual, even startling it was to come upon a cemetery in the middle of the city. I may have taken to it simply because it was so easy to overlook, like a tiny clue. Yet it has been where it is for centuries. All one needs to do is notice it, as I do now, again. Atop the low wall on either side of the iron gate out front, on a six-inch ledge, lie small stones and seashells. They seem deliberately placed, perhaps as signs of respect.

ALL THAT I am, all that we are, will come to nothing. Think of that. This frozen skin, this pile of bones, these tears, these flying dreams, ferocious glee, careless whims, these dark ambitions and darker memories, and recriminations, darker still. All to nothing. In one moment, our squalling birth. In the next, the death of our regrets. Our minds are peopled by entire civilizations, which will be gone, just like that. Just like *that*. When we die, history dies. Can you believe it? Our songs. Even our songs. Even this thought. Perish the thought.

Is there a roaring after this? A blast of light? Something, anything that might serve as a postscript? P.S., Kilroy, we were here. Would it not greatly gratify us to be like a star and live in our own afterburn? I don't know. The eventual streets and avenues that lie before me today, to which I shall proceed.

And the citizens yet to be encountered. And the impressive edifices yet to be remarked upon, and surveyed in wonder. They live in nothing until I approach. So it is possible to exist in nothing. Don't you think? One can remove the owls and the tulips, and all the glories of the earth, amen, and have them still. My temples ache.

The sweetest thought is the smile of a girl in a dress with pale yellow florets, who walks toward me at the end of a summer evening, when the sun, done with lighting beech trees, larks, and the lot, hunches its shoulders along the disappearing line. She, then, assumes the sun's role. Hard to believe, but it is true . . . Hard to believe that she too will come to nothing. Do we leave a trace? Only after you speak do I know what you mean.

THE BODY IS that of a normally developed white male, measuring seventy inches in length and weighing 175 pounds, and appearing generally consistent with his age, as given, of seventy-one years. The body is cold to the touch and uninvolved with declining rigor mortis. There is no lividity. X-rays suggest several former fractures to the left shoulder, the right cheekbone, the fifth cervical vertebra, as well as multiple wounds of undetermined origins to the heart. Toxology reveals traces of Advil, Prilosec, and Lipitor, and food fragments indicating a poorly balanced diet, if said diet could be defined as balanced at all. Anomaly: as coroner was about to cover the body and place it back in the file cabinet, it sat up straight, smiled, said "It isn't over yet," and sang "Daisy, Daisy." This made it difficult to determine cause of death.

IT WAS ONE thing to wander the streets like a shadow, shadowing shady people. Silent, stealthy. How divinely removed it felt to be driven by a suspicion of everything, wondering if all things bright and beautiful were in fact bright and beautiful, or if I peeled them down to the nub like an onion, would they show themselves to be black at the core, themselves shadows of shadows in the city of mystery, mixing and matching, as shadows do, without the ability to speak.

But it was quite another thing to wonder if that wandering would ever come to an end, the illimitable walk reaching its limits, or would I become like Cain, with no wind disclosing my whereabouts. I would never be considered a missing person, since no one would report me missing because there would have been no place for me to be missing from, and therefore I would not be missing, officially. For who would be there in nowhere to report me missing? Who would be nowhere to indicate I was ever a person?

And it was a third thing to imagine where I would be if I were to move among the objects, the suspects, of my wandering, as someone who never would return to the world that might have been interested in them, and then might act upon information about them—to discover all that I had discovered, and thus punish the guilty and free the innocent, and reward me for my keen eyes and ears, but instead of all that, to blend in with the targets of my scrutiny, knowing that I had no authority to turn them in. I would be one of them, powerless. A shadow like them. Me and my shadow, walking down the avenue.

And if that were so, would I then identify with all whom I pursued, being one of them, and drop my standards and my guard, because I would know how it felt to live under a microscope, or a magnifying glass, to be precise? Probably not. I think not. I know me. I was the world in which I walked. Though I was assured there would be no returning from my wanderings to the land of light and judgment, I trust that I would continue to shadow the shadows anyway, for even in the world of the lost there are those who know what must be done, and I would be one of those persons, missing or not. And that was the fourth thing.

ODD TO SAY, but in New York even the lost do not seem lost. Years ago, when we were living on the Upper West Side, I did a little work with a project for the homeless. Clients were given medical treatment. Some held jobs. Most drifted in and out of the shelter. One woman lived in a tree in Central Park. All seemed relatively content with their lot.

One afternoon, a fellow named Charlie, whom I knew from the shelter, decided to set up a living room on the sidewalk in front of a church on Eighty-sixth and Amsterdam. He had scavenged in the area and had selected a fake Oriental rug, an orange couch, a Barcalounger, two folding chairs, and an end table on which he placed a lamp plugged into nothing. The place looked pretty good. Walking past Charlie's outdoor living room, I thought I would join him. We sat facing each other discussing this and that. After a while, he stretched and looked bored. "Well, Roger," he said. "I've enjoyed this little chat. But I'm expecting guests."

THE OTHER DAY, in the memoir class, a man of, say, seventy who was writing about himself at age ten, described an episode when he had a friend over and his father, whose mind was going fast, had pissed his pants on the stairs. The friend fled hurriedly, and the boy, confused and unable to help his dad, retreated to the TV to watch *Casbah,* which was playing on Million Dollar Movie. Peter and I watched *Casbah* together, too, perhaps at the very same time as that student of mine, and we watched it day after day for a week. That was the appealing feature of Million Dollar Movie. It played one movie, all day, every day, for a week.

So we sat together, afternoon and night, as Tony Martin, playing the master thief Pepe Le Moko, pursued a dark-eyed beauty whose name I forget, as he himself was pursued by Yvonne de Carlo, playing Inez, who loved Pepe unrequitedly, and by Peter Lorre, who played a cop named Slimane. Le Moko was safe from Slimane as long as he remained in the labyrinth of the Casbah, so Slimane arranged for the dark-eyed beauty to lure him out. I also forget how.

But I still can sing every word of the song Martin sang, about man being meant for woman and woman for man. And I still can see Yvonne de Carlo yearning for him, as he yearned for another, who offered him only imprisonment. And if I had been paying attention, I would have understood the story as a parable about a man unable to avoid the pursuit of his own destruction. But instead I focused on the casbah and how wonderful it must have been to live there forever, in secret.

I'll tell you a secret. The children of Gramercy Park stumbled upon a defunct mine shaft from the era of the Gramercy Silver Lode, back in the 1830s, fell in, and did not return. Keep this to yourself. Much was made of the mysterious event at the time, and search parties composed of deputized residents combed the park and its environs for several weeks afterward. But no one could find the mine shaft that swallowed up the children, although for many days one could hear their voices carried in the hedges and the oak trees of Gramercy Park, and in the pillars of clouds that rose over the neighborhood. Loud and excited at first, the voices soon grew faint, during which time the search parties scoured the park inch by inch, frantic that the children's voices would disappear altogether and leave no sound to follow. This, in fact, happened. After a few more days, nothing was heard of the children of Gramercy Park ever again, and for a great many years the park was occupied only by grown-ups, as the neighborhood was childless.

The president of the Gramercy Park Association, upon consulting with the membership, proposed that a memorial be established to honor the missing children. Two years passed, and the matter was hotly debated at the National Arts Club by the neighborhood grown-ups, some of whom thought a bench with a bronze plaque would be appropriate, while others envisioned the sculpting of a statue of a child placed in front of the club, bearing a forlorn expression to symbolize all the children who had fallen into the mine shaft. Still others held out for a smaller version of the wall memorializing those lost in the Vietnam War, in Washington, D.C., to emphasize the solemnity of the occasion. But then it was pointed out that those who had heard the voices of the disappeared children reported they had sounded happy, exultant even. No one thought it proper to erect a memorial to exultant missing children, so the discussion reverted to the memorial bench.

It has been sixty years since the children of Gramercy

Park disappeared, and as yet no memorial bench has been placed in the park. Most of the residents who remember the children at all doubt that there ever will be any memorial to them. Since that time, other children slowly have returned to the park, and today one hardly can tell the current Gramercy Park from the one I played in. But Teddy Welles isn't there anymore, or Pete Krulewich, or Larry Hunt, or Ira Fink, Ruddy Platt, or Spike Abbott, or Bruce Morrell, or Chick Jacobson, or the Vercessi boys, or Jay Westcott, or Parnell Gunn. And Mark and Johnny Morris are not there either. We all fell into a mine shaft, and nothing was heard of us again.

THAT STORY IS made up, as you suspected, but not wholly made up, as it involves certain accuracies within a whopper of a lie. Here, students, is where fact and fiction meld. And a memoir may make use of either or both. If I wanted to, I could tell you that my brother, for all his frailty and shyness, was a rabid tennis player who gave not an inch on the court, and who, often as not, would aim a forehand at an opponent's nuts. Or that my father was a secret drinker—gin, mostly, to keep the booze off his breath as he examined patients. Or that my mother had been a belly dancer in the 1920s in a Negro nightclub, in Newark. Not that any of that is true. But I could put it all in a novel, and, believe it or not, in a memoir as well. By the time you've told any story, fact or fiction, well enough, you've made it up anyway. And if the odd fragments of information I just detailed were consistent with the entire pictures I have drawn of my brother, mother, and father, why not use them?

I do not urge you, or even encourage you, to toss wholesale lies into your memoirs—though not out of some ethical compunction on my part, or a fear that you'll be caught in your lies and pilloried or sued. Rather, that the lies (because it is their way) are liable to overtake the facts of your story and run away with it. That you do not want. But a fanciful touch here and there? The fanciful touch, if effective and original, functions as an extension of the truth, a dreaming into the truth. Did I tell you that my grandfather Patta used to sit Indian-style atop the brick chimney of his tenement roof, wearing a fez and puffing on a hookah, watching smoke circles rise through his folded legs? Just messin' with you.

ALLOW ME A true story I've told elsewhere. It comes to me because it's about childhood and detectives, though I did not see that when I told it originally, or actually, until now. How the wandering mind works. From the age of ten or so, I developed the irritating penchant of slipping quotes from movies into a normal conversation. Those with whom I was speaking had no idea why a movie line had been introduced, but they recognized that by doing so I was indicating less of an interest in what we were saying than in amusing myself. You may imagine how this practice enhanced my already hectic social life.

At a dance in high school, I approached my best friend, Peter Valente, who was standing in front of, and nearly concealing, a plumpish girl known to us both. I greeted Valente with a line from *Beau Brummell* in which Stewart Granger had insulted George III by speaking of him to another party, as though the king were not present. "Who's your fat friend?" said Granger of the king. I said the same thing to Valente. The hidden girl stepped forward, steaming. How could I explain that I was speaking of George III?

That was the sort of line I would quote. And if I were patient, I usually would find a conversational slot in which it fit. A line I *never* got in came from the movie *Earthquake,* one of the disaster movies of the 1970s. The plot involved a villain who was stalking a young woman. One would think that the prospect of an earthquake would have been enough to distract him. But the man was focused. When the earthquake finally hit, he jumped the woman. George Kennedy—who played a cop because he usually played a cop—pulled the guy off her and shot him dead. Then he said to the woman: "I don't know what it is. Earthquakes seem to bring out the worst in some guys." The only place I could think of where that line might have worked was California.

Which brings me to the line that took me thirty years to

find a home for, but it happened. It was delivered by Nigel Bruce as Dr. Watson in one of the Basil Rathbone *Sherlock Holmes* movies I saw on TV. Watson wanted to impress a couple who did not know of Holmes or his exploits. "Haven't you heard of the giant rat of Sumatra?" he asked them, referring to one of Holmes's sensational cases. In "The Adventure of the Sussex Vampire," Holmes delivers the line a bit differently: "Matilda Briggs was not the name of a young woman, Watson. It was a ship which is associated with the giant rat of Sumatra, a story for which the world is not yet prepared." I chose to use the movie line. "Haven't you heard of the giant rat of Sumatra?" It was tricky. There had to be an opening for the surprise at someone's ignorance, also for the rat, and of course, its size.

Then one day in 1978, I was lunching with friends, and it happened to be the fiftieth anniversary of the creation of Mickey Mouse. I barely was paying attention to the table talk, when someone asked, "Has there ever been a bigger rodent?"

THE FIRST OF two times I actually saw Basil Rathbone was in Kennebunkport, Maine. I was with my parents and Peter, and we were taking a tour of the town. As we were walking down a stone embankment to the beach, Basil Rathbone was walking up. He was dressed in slacks and a collared shirt, though without the deerstalker's hat or the pipe. We smiled.

He smiled. I didn't ask him if he enjoyed playing Sherlock Holmes, because I thought he *was* Sherlock Holmes. I didn't say a word.

And I didn't speak to him the second time either, when I caught sight of him in the Indian Walk children's shoes store on Madison Avenue. This time I was there just with my dad. As we walked in, Basil Rathbone was walking out, once again he and I passing like consulting detectives in the night. It seemed odd to me that he was in a children's shoes store without a child, but I figured he was on a case, which was another reason I never would have presumed to speak to him. I imagined he thought the same thing about me.

THINK OF THE names in small print at the end of a movie, after the end to be precise, when the movie is done and the audience shuffles out, turning their backs on the names that roll down forever, so fast you can hardly read them, yet they count for something. All the people it takes to make a movie. Eventually, though it lasts many minutes, and hundreds and hundreds of names are displayed, they are gone. And here they come now, down Thirty-seventh Street, my fellow citizens, extras, my fellow walkers, who have slid off the screen at the end of the movie and have filled the streets around me. How they multiply.

What, I wonder, did Noah make of the sight of his passengers when the waters finally receded and they spilled out onto dry land, and two became four became hundreds. Billions. When the crowd got out of hand, Noah may have had trouble recalling exactly what his role had been in the repopulation of the earth. He was six hundred years old, after all. Similarly, I stand in wonder at all the people of my world, and how many of them it takes to make a movie.

CUE THE PEDESTRIANS on their way up First, in the direction of the UN building. I do not follow. I have little interest in nations, united or otherwise. Besides, detective work when applied to nations means espionage, and nothing could bore me more than espionage. Who cares about the crimes of governments? You can't solve them, and much of the time, that's what governments do anyway—commit crimes. Crimes with little variety. As clients, governments will always let you down, and when you think you've done the right thing for this government or that, you soon will be shown that it was the wrong thing, because there is no side to take in government but that of government itself. In espionage, detectives are merely spies. No one weeps for spies. No one cares. I could take every one of John le Carré's so-called heroes in all their gray, bleak, self-congratulatory splendor, and toss them in the drink, just east of the United Nations building. The only time the UN served a good mystery was in *North by Northwest*,

and even then it merely provided a lofty setting for an ordinary stab in the back. Real detectives do not go to the United
Nations building. I keep my distance.

INSTEAD, I VEER toward the cold comfort of Murray Hill,
whose boundaries are Thirty-fourth Street to Fortieth, and
Madison Avenue to Third. I see the area now as then, not as
a neighborhood really, but as a loose collection of city blocks
with pretty town houses, pastel colors, browns, pinks, and
light grays, each standing in a distracted elegance. Window
boxes, flowerless in winter. Gleaming doors. Windows tall
or round, like portholes. And Sniffin Court, on Thirty-sixth
Street between Third and Lex, an enclave of two facing rows
of lovely carriage-house-size homes, with a slate path running between them. Neither snooty nor familiar, the houses
of Murray Hill tend to their own business.

This was uptown New York in the nineteenth century.
J. P. Morgan built his mansion here, at Thirty-sixth and Madison, a portion of which became the Morgan Library. In the
eighteenth century, the land was a farm belonging to a mer-
chant, Robert Murray, covering twenty-nine acres, rising to a
hill at Thirty-fourth Street and sloping toward Forty-second
and Lex. Crops were grown on some of the estates, but their
main purpose simply was to be admired. Ginny and I were
married in Murray Hill, in the Unitarian Community Church

at Thirty-fifth between Madison and Park. As religions go, Unitarianism seemed to have few standards, making it suitable for us.

For anyone in the detective trade the best thing about Murray Hill was Philo Vance, the courtly, effete, haughty, overeducated, overdressed consulting detective, created by S. S. Van Dine. And just as the name S. S. Van Dine is unbelievable, unless it also is the name of a steamship, Vance, too, was a story for which the world was not prepared, or ever would be. He had an apartment on East Thirty-eighth Street, with a roof garden, and a manservant named Curry. Van Dine described him as "a marked Nordic type," with an aquiline nose and gray, wide eyes, and a mouth that displayed "cynical cruelty." He was a three-handicap golfer, a champion archer and polo player, a master at poker, and a connoisseur of fine wine, food, and Chinese ceramics and tapestries. He was "largely educated in Europe," whatever that meant. He smoked Régie cigarettes, whatever they were. As a boy, I barely understood a word Vance said. He swore, "My word!" and "By Jove!" He came out with things like "I shouldn't miss it for all the lost comedies of Menander!"

But he was so damn smart. *The Bishop Murder Case, The Benson Murder Case, The Kennel, The Greene, The Scarab, The Canary* murder cases, and more. Using not ratiocination but rather "his knowledge of human psychology," he brought evildoers to their knees. And every crime occurred in the wealthy houses of New York, fancier than Gramercy Park but close enough for me to recognize the places where secret sins abounded and motives remained in hiding behind substantial closed doors. I might have been Vance, I thought, minus the affectations—the man apart who is aware of the terrors people are capable of, and of the justice that awaits them, solving the mysteries of the world and then returning to my home with a rooftop garden on East Thirty-eighth Street.

YET THERE WERE times in the dream of days when I patrolled Murray Hill looking at the lovely houses with casual melancholy, knowing that the happy and sophisticated faces therein could never be mine. The sky was a gray silence, and the fires flared in the slits of the drapes. And all sorts of clever talk transpired therein, and all sorts of exciting news was announced, and confidence contained each house like skin. But these things were not mine. The families who lived with such stately ebullience did not belong to me. And so, while I stared at the great windows, tall as medieval towers, or at the lower level kitchens, blazing with their brass pots caressed in the thick arms of cook, arms glistening with sweat, my heart leapt from joy to envy thence to despair.

For even as I coveted, I knew that the lives that seemed like glittering smiles would inevitably be revealed with a parting of the drapes as no less drab than my own. When I walked on, the moon would swing away toward stone villages else-where, and the stars as well, and I would be left bearing the weight of darkness. And in that—writer detective, detective writer—I felt at home.

EVERY BLOCK AROUND here has a history, but you can't see history. Dashiell Hammett, who moved around a lot, lived at 155 East Thirtieth when he was writing *The Glass Key*. At 19 East Thirty-first, the Herald Square Hotel, were the of-fices of *Life*—not the picture magazine but rather a sophisti-cated humor magazine, whose name was bought by Time Inc. in 1936. The Herald Square Hotel was also where Charles Dana Gibson created the fashionable "Gibson Girl." The golden cherub above the doorway is flanked by the words *Wit* and *Humor.*

At the corner of Thirty-third Street and Park stands a Lewis Mumford skyscraper, built in 1927. Ayn Rand worked as a typist here while researching *The Fountainhead.* Rand lived at 120 East Thirty-fourth, till her death in 1982. In *The Age of Innocence,* Newland Archer moves to East Thirty-ninth Street after his marriage. The publisher Charles Scribner lived at 64 East Thirty-fourth. Henry Miller lived in the area. Enrico Caruso, too, briefly.

It's nice to know the history of these streets, but the pres-ent crowds out the past. The least interesting-looking pedestrian pushes Ayn Rand, Caruso, even Hammett out of my thoughts. There is a great deal of history in New York, but, as they say, nothing like the present. One feels the breath of history in places like Boston and Philadelphia. Not here. The present is the tense of the city. Tonight, you are here-and-now. Me, too.

THAT PLACE WE lived in on the Upper West Side was on the second story of a brownstone on Eighty-seventh. The downstairs apartment was occupied by a woman in her thirties whose working routine was known to Ginny and me—out by eight in the morning, back by six. She was a pleasant neighbor. We greeted one another by name, but were no more familiar than that.

One morning, as I was walking our dog, I noticed that the woman's apartment door was wide open and the lights were on. It was well after eight, but I presumed nothing was amiss, even after I returned from my dog walk twenty minutes later. An hour or so after that, Ginny and I were headed out when I glanced at the woman's apartment, which remained as it had been earlier. Door wide open, lights on. I called her name. Nothing. Louder. Still nothing. Hesitantly, I approached her door and called her name again. When there was no response this time, I decided to look inside, full of trepidation. The apartment was lit brightly. A PBS coffee mug on the counter. A yellow bowl with remnants of corn flakes or Special K clinging to the sides. A beige bra drooped over a ladder-back chair. An unmade bed. No one in the bathroom. And no young woman, dead or alive. She'd probably been in a rush that morning and left the door open.

But I tell you, poking around that apartment, which is what detectives and police do all the time, was chilling. It was entering someone else's life and all of the accoutrements peculiar to that life. And while it is exhilarating to do the very same thing as a writer of fiction, when you have created a person and the apartment out of the materials of your mind, to snoop around in reality makes you feel like the lowest sort of intruder. You are where you are not supposed to be, not invited or welcome. And whether or not the worst that you feared comes to pass, you feel ashamed, as though you had committed a crime yourself. That evening I told the woman what had happened, and what I'd done. She thanked me and shrugged it off. Whenever I spoke with her after that day, however, I made it brief.

WHY IS MEMORY more self-punishing than approving? A woman I ran into some years ago, the sister of a boy from the neighborhood, told me she had never forgotten a day when the kids were choosing up sides for a softball game. No one would take her because she was a girl, she said, and I had welcomed her to my team. And recently, a man who wanted me to join him in some money venture (I didn't) tried to persuade me by recalling my reckless bravery as a boy on an occasion when I fought a Third Avenue thug who was pushing us around and pinned him to the sidewalk. I had no recollection of either incident.

What I do remember is a feeling of remorse every time I found myself in a fistfight—win, lose, or draw—and many more instances of cowardice than bravery. If someone else's memory paints me as generous and courageous, and my own memory thinks much less of me, it might mean that I am better than my self-assessment for the very severity of my self-criticism. Then again, if I am right and they are not, I could be even worse than I imagine for deliberately forgetting a slew of sins. In any event, the competition is not among truths. It is among memories—some woman's, some man's, versus mine. Does all this mean that the "who am I" question is up for grabs? I prefer to think that who we are depends not on scraps of information tossed up by a perception of the past, but rather on present actions, which wards off memory in the interests of simply doing. See? If no one believed in time, this wouldn't even be a problem. You are what you are now, the eternal now, unencumbered by high or low expectations informed by memory, which is untrustworthy anyway.

Now, *this* comes back: a kid in summer camp, sort of a henchman to the bunk bully, who had persuaded himself that he was as tough and strong as the bully he served. One night he decided to try out his imagined prowess on me. He jumped on my back and started to punch me in the neck. I got him in a headlock. "Give!" I told him. He did not surrender. His face reddened. "Give!" I repeated. Harder, tighter, relishing my shameful victory. He gave.

HERE'S A MEMORY so faint it arises as a palimpsest, present and absent. It involves a Halloween party. But that is the only fact it involves. The event itself—was it Halloween?—is associated with the scent of creosote. And the people—was I there?—were dour and disapproving. Something to do with a mask of the Frankenstein monster, I think. Or of President Eisenhower. Ike. Ice. Maybe it wasn't a party. All that is left is a feeling of being out of place. But that could be anywhere.

Oh, pay no attention to me. I was just another lost boy, a lot luckier than most. Better that I pay you a visit, inquire as to your health, read something to you, if you like, until you fall asleep. I could read to you during your sleep. Several years ago, I read to a girl in a coma. The fifteen-year-old daughter of a friend had been hit by a car and medivaced to the ICU. She lay in her white bed like a princess under a spell. I read her *Crime and Punishment* (I have no idea why) and wondered when she awoke, if she would call for Dostoyevsky or demand never to hear his name again. Neither occurred. When she did awaken at last, we all were too grateful to worry about her education in Russian literature. Not that I ever finished *Crime and Punishment* myself. Every time I try, I get only as far as the *Crime*.

As for loneliness, I exaggerate it. My troubles were my own, but no different in size or depth from that of any kid. Everyone bears a burden. And mine were pretty lightweight. In the mid 1970s, I wrote a weekly column for the *Washington Post*. Standing at the urinal one day beside Howard Simons, the *Post*'s managing editor, I said, "Howard, why does one pronounce the *n* in *columnist,* but not in the word *column*? Shouldn't *columnist* be pronounced without the *n*? *Columist*?" Without looking up, he said, "Roger, I wish I had your problems."

BUT *YOU*, PAL. How are you feeling these days? The docs assured you that you'd be on your feet in no time. And here you are, on your feet, yet worried to death about the matter of no time. Should we speak of every topic but radiation? Or should we speculate about how much radiation you have absorbed, comparing you to the citizens of Hiroshima, and calculating that you may have been given the bigger dose? We could share a good laugh over that. You know? You touch my heart. Do you realize that?

Here, then, I pause, and imagine you, in your sorrowful beauty and your low, lovely voice. What are you doing out there among the shady characters? Will you speak in my dreams and walk down the street ahead of me, knowing I am behind you, yet never turning to face me? Athens comes to mind, and I see Mount Lycabettus at Easter and you in the silent spiral of pilgrims' candles in the night. What is your role on this random walk? I sit at a small round table covered with a checkered cloth, in the back of the café, in my trench coat, with my fedora angled over my eyes, pulling on a Marlboro and watching you admiringly. You have endured so much. Are you there?

A WORD IN favor of policemen? No one will admit it, but without the presence of the get-everything-wrong cops, detectives could not get anything right. Not only is it the policeman who first deals with the corpse (position of, nature of wound, autopsy, etc.), but it is also he who gives us everyone who did *not* do it, thus, in effect, becoming the ass-backward advocate of Holmes's explanation to Watson in *The Sign of Four,* that "when you have eliminated the impossible, whatever remains, however improbable, must be the truth."

Yet outside these purely functional attributes is the policeman himself, his official drudgery, his glamourless heroism. At one point in *The Maltese Falcon,* the head cop berates an underling for not being thorough enough—"So, ya seen your duty and ya done it." But that's just it about cops. They see their duty and they do it. And, while the best moments of any mystery, including the solution, are given to the outsider detective, it is the civil servant cop who keeps the laws in place and maintains civilization, such as it is, not for a single flashy case, but every day, day after day. Who would want a world made up solely of Philo Vances? I wonder what it would be like to end a mystery story, not with a wisecrack or a self-satisfied remark of the great detective, but instead with a shot of the cop hauling away the killer the detective discovered, and cuffing him, and printing him, and locking him up. Or better, a shot of him going home well after the story is finished, and Holmes or Wolfe has already raised a glass to his own genius, and we see the dog-tired policeman lay his gun and badge on top of his dresser and strip down to his civvies, and turn on *Dancing with the Stars*.

INTERESTING, THAT SO many detectives speak peculiarly. Vance's fancy patter was barely intelligible. Poirot said, "Never will my English be quite perfect," and he was always tossing in French phrases to make his point. Holmes's English was frequently snotty, archly witty. Sam Spade spit out English through his teeth. Charlie Chan hardly spoke it at all, resorting to the wisdom of Confucius and other aphorisms, and speaking a pidgin English that had no use for *a, an,* or

the. In *Murder by Death* (1976), which burlesqued all the famous detectives, a talking moose head on a wall was so exas-
perated with Chan's English, he yelled out, "Use the article!"

On the other hand, you tend to pay attention to these
oddly speaking characters, more than you might if they talked
like everyone else. It's like writing, again. What you want to
do as a writer, above all, is to find your original language,
which, like the detective, allows you your own way to get at
the truth. A real writer's language sounds like no one else's.
It is as if he sees the world so strangely that he must find an
equally strange way to express himself.

BUT WHAT IS one to make of the Jacobsons? Of Chick Jacobson, né Solomon Jacobson, and his sisters, Ruth and Edie,
and his little brother, Dick? I ask only because the Jacobson
family was an anomaly in the neighborhood, where almost everyone else was upper-middle-class WASP, or wannabees, or
wanna-appears, like my dad. The Jacobsons were evidently,
openly, aggressively, very very Jewish. They looked Jewish.
They sounded Jewish. They celebrated Jewish holidays, including Purim. They let other people who were Jewish and
didn't know it, know it. I am speaking of me and Chick in the
park one afternoon, when he informed me emphatically that
I was Jewish. I was six, maybe seven, and had no idea what
he was talking about. "Oh yeah," he said. "You're Jewish."

When I went home, I asked my mom, who made a sweet, affirming smile.

So naturally, my dad would have nothing to do with the Jacobsons. Neither with the kids, who were sharp and giving and full of life, nor with the mother, a small, kind, pale, silver-haired woman with a tired face, nor with the father, a gentle, burly guy who owned an antiques shop specializing in monstrosities—outlandish chandeliers and huge carved wooden chairs made for Norse gods. So naturally, I hung out with the Jacobsons. Whole weekends were spent in their apartment at 60 Gramercy, which was crowded with the junk from Mr. Jacobson's shop. Loud and loving. Such a strange family.

Unlike myself or the other kids I played with who lived around the park, Chick went to the local public school and, afterward, to Stuyvesant High School, which at the time was located on the east side of Stuyvesant Park. By then he and I had diverged, as kids do, though for a few years, Chick was my constant friend. I ate dinners at his house two or three times a week. Sloppy dishes of noodles and pummeled meat, consumed noisily while the family quarreled one moment and made extravagant plans the next. Chick didn't know how to pronounce *yacht*. He referred to a "yackt." He didn't care. He had confidence in himself. All the Jacobsons had confidence in themselves and in one another, which made one happy to be in their presence. They feared nothing, those Jacobsons.

SPEAKING OF JEWS—and who does not?—since my father had refused a bar mitzvah when he was a boy, I insisted on having one. My determination was born of nothing more spiritual than a wish to give him an in-your-face gesture of rebellion—a gesture made more pointless by my father's reaction to it, which was simply to accede. He did not even blink when the synagogue I chose was the Spanish and Portuguese, probably because I remembered the cemetery on Eleventh Street. I had no idea that the temple, which occupied a monumental gray building on Seventieth Street and Central Park West, was one of the oldest Orthodox synagogues in the country. Thus, merely to stick it to my old man, I undertook instruction in the strictest and most demanding branch of Judaism, creating a series of hurdles for myself, such as trying to learn to read Hebrew in less than a year.

In fact, I couldn't do it, so I decided to memorize the part of the Torah I was assigned to present. In the dark afternoons after school, I rode the bus to the synagogue, muttering my Hebrew recitation like an old man in prayer. On my bar mitzvah morning, I stood on an elegant wooden platform at the center of the temple, beside the white-bearded David de Sola Pool and four other solemn rabbis in black, as I pretended to read the Hebrew before me. At one point, I pronounced an important word inaccurately, and the rabbis shook with stifled laughter. No one ever told me what terrible mistake I had made, but it must have been a beaut.

When the ceremony was over, I stood outside with my family and their friends, and with my own friends, including Chick. I received warm wishes and congratulations and kisses, as I nodded and chatted and felt like the fraud I was. Except for weddings and bar mitzvahs and bat mizvahs of the children of our friends today, that morning at the Spanish and Portuguese was the last time I ever set foot in a synagogue. What is worse, I knew it would be when the inspiration of a bar mitzvah had first occurred to me. I gained nothing by it. My father . . . I see him standing before the three stone columns of the synagogue, wearing his derby hat and black winter coat with the Chesterfield collar. My father smiled knowingly. That night, I buried myself in the couch, wolfed down a BLT, and watched Claude Rains in *The Invisible Man* on TV.

How I wish I felt the affection for my neighborhood that Alfred Kazin felt for his, in Brooklyn, in *A Walker in the City*. Much of Kazin's love of place came from streets like Pitkin Avenue in Brownsville, teeming with people and surprises. More was due to the Jewishness of the area. Though he described his intimacy with his synagogue as "loveless," still it gave him a feeling of belonging, of occupying a niche in a tradition. Not long ago, I asked Leon Wieseltier about the core of his own passion for Judaism. He said his love for it is profound, because it allows him to explore spiritual and meta-physical questions, issues of meaning. So his Judaism is not solely collective, it is idiosyncratically individuated. His joy derives from the poetry and the philosophy as much as from the people. Judaism is both his religion and civilization, he told me. I am happy for him, but such a passion never could have been mine. My father saw to that. So did Gramercy Park, which for all its insistent bourgeoisie dignity remained joyless even at Christmas, when the tree blazed in the park with its familiar set of lights and the accordionist from Calvary Church led residents in the routinized singing of carols.

I was literary editor of the *New Republic* in the mid 1970s, and in that time I had dealings with Alfred Kazin, which was akin to waltzing with a learned Jewish polar bear: equally impressive, cute, and dangerous. Alfred wrote several book reviews for the magazine, all perfect. Then one morning, he phoned to ask if he could review Lillian Hellman's latest autobiography. Being in my early thirties, and having not a clue as to any of the internecine wars waged by the older literary set—and not a whiff of suspicion that Kazin hated Hellman as he alone could hate—I said sure. The review arrived still smoking. It was a raging personal attack from the first sentence on, rarely stooping to discuss the contents of the book. I told Alfred I couldn't run it. He told me I was depriving him of his rights of free expression. I told him, bullshit.

During the following months, whenever I ran into anyone

in journalism or publishing, that person would report, "You know, Alfred Kazin says you deprived him of his rights of free expression." Then Alfred called again, and said he was coming to Washington, where our family lived at the time and where the *New Republic* was located. Would I have lunch with him? We had not been seated ten seconds when he said, "You deprived me of my rights of free expression." This time I said, "Alfred. I probably have a longer life ahead of me than you do. Tell me. Are you ever going to get over this?" He laughed good-naturedly, giving every indication that the matter was closed. Later in the week, I got a call from an editor at the *New York Times* Sunday Arts section. "Alfred Kazin says you deprived him of his rights of free expression. Do you have any comment?"

Like many crazy writers, Kazin was a lot easier to read than to live with. In his prose, I still hear his high-pitched smoky voice relating his walk in the city, glorying in a Brooklyn summer day and in the "indescribable joy" he felt being himself in his neighborhood, which wrapped around him like a mother's arms. That I did envy.

THE SNOW WAS blinding, but I had to get there. You understand. I had lost the formula. So I plowed into the blizzard wearing bandages covering my body and my face, my whole head, and the obvious garish wig and my outer-space sunglasses. At the inn I demanded a room and pored over my notes from the lab, muttering, "There must be a way back." But then the bobbies burst in and offered me sushi. O tempura. O mores. In daylight you cannot see me, but in a blizzard I appear a bubble. "There must be a way back." Stop me before I sleep again, because as I've said before, an invisible man can rule the world. And vice versa. Definitely vice versa.

EVERY SO OFTEN one reads of a man or a woman who takes a walk across the country, or the continent, or even someone who walks around the world, over the Poles. Feats of endurance and stamina, to be sure, but not real walks, as I understand them. The man who walks around the world must be conscious, all the time, of just how far he has traveled, and of how far he has to go. He measures his heartbeats, monitors his pulse. Such thoughts do not occur to the wanderer, the one who has no interest in setting world records or in drawing attention to himself. He occasionally may be aware of how tired he has grown, but he is no more self-conscious than that. He looks away from himself. He wonders.

He is like Freddie, Margie's boyfriend on the TV show *My Little Margie.* Margie's father had no use for Freddie, because Freddie didn't have a job. He spent his days watching people work at construction sites, and he was completely happy.

Praise to those who walk around the world. Praise to those who measure their meters and miles. But the highest praise to that fellow here on Sixteenth and Union Square East, in the green parka and the yellow boots, who wanders past, looking at me looking at him. And, it goes without saying, praise to Freddie.

BUT WHAT'S WRONG with *him,* who seems intentionally to have driven his shoulder into mine on his path straight to hell? I don't want to know. I don't want to hear about his overbearing boss, or his idiot brother-in-law, or his ungrateful children or his lover who has unrequited him for the umpteenth time this week. I want nothing to do with him and his furious life, or to listen to him as he collars me and shouts, "What do *you* know of suffering or want or the dry hunger I have felt for her all this time—she who feels fire only for other men? I could kill her. I could kill *you*." And if I were foolish enough to give him the time of day, I would then ask, "Why me?" And he would say, "Because you deserve to die." Yeah yeah.

On the ice-pocked plain of Fifteenth Street between Second and Third, there is much to be angry about. The man in the too-long camel's hair coat is angry about his great aunt, of all people. The man in the white-tooled cowboy boots is angry about his insurance company, which has cancelled his coverage after the fender bender. The woman at his side is angry at him for the fender bender. And both are angry at me because I am not going anywhere and thus appear at peace. And the one who crashed into my shoulder may be angry at me for the same reason. But I still don't want to hear about it. This aimlessness, I find, drives some people up the wall. Good.

A murdered boy is buried in the foundation of the Greek Orthodox church near Twenty-second Street and Third. How would I have detected that without my illimitable walk, I ask you?

ABOUT HATRED AND ANGER. They have no effect on their objects. They are real and virulent enough to you. But no one else feels them very long, and certainly not as long or as deeply as you do. All you have done by generating such weapons is to add to the vast hatred and anger of the world, which indirectly ends in the deaths of millions. Do you really want to commit second-degree mass murder all your life? This message is brought to you by the society for preventive detection.

Once there was a boy who walked and walked. And where he walked the streets curled skyward and the trees went flat as dishes. Birds roared, beetles went about their business, and the tulips conversed with poets. All this occurred, and more, where the boy walked.

FOUR THEORIES ABOUT the nature of a perfect crime. The first has it that the perfect crime is one in which you get away with murder. You did it, all right, but you don't get caught. Say, you had an airtight alibi. Or better, that you had no motive for the act, like Leopold and Loeb, who did not know their little boy victim personally but simply wanted to commit the perfect crime. They might have got away with it, if not for their egotistical personalities. They were too intent on having others appreciate their brilliance—a very bad move for criminals seeking perfection.

The second theory is that the perfect crime is one in which someone else is caught and punished for what you did. That way, everyone thinks the crime has been solved, case closed—everyone but you and the patsy you set up to take the fall. There's a nice neatness to this sort of crime, especially if the real murderer confronts the falsely convicted with no one else present, on death row, for example, moments before the execution. At this point, it would be lovely to see the innocent man strangle the guilty so that divine justice might be served. Alas, in the realm of terrestrial justice, no one would know that the guilty party got his. All anyone would think is that the wronged man killed twice.

Which brings us to the third theory—that the perfect crime is one in which the murderer dies without anyone knowing that he did it. Agatha Christie's *Ten Little Indians,* its title cleaned up from the original *Ten Little Niggers,* shows us a vengeful judge who knocks off ten victims, including himself. If the murderer dies without anyone knowing he did

it, the crime may be seen as perfect, if somewhat unsatisfy-
ing for the mastermind. Go to the trouble of committing the
perfect crime and you deserve to see the fruits of your labor.

And here is where the fourth and final theory comes in, in
that it involves the crime you commit, and see, and everyone
sees, and nothing is done about it. I refer to the crime you committed when you walked past the wounded or when you failed
to attend the depressed. Why, you clever bastard, you did it
without leaving even a partial fingerprint, without any telltale
ballistics. You did it without a trace. The crime of no passion.
No witnesses. No body. And here's the beauty of it. The world
lies dead at your feet and no one knows you did it, not even the
dead. Sweet.

ENCLOSED FIND RECEIPTS from Mayfair Hotel in Dover,
Delaware, as well as plane tickets to and from San Antonio,
and a handwritten note from Ming, the owner of Ming's in
Seattle, in lieu of a formal receipt, stating that I spent $23
on a below-average mei fun dinner, plus a $4 tip for Ming's
son, Ming Junior. Find also six receipts for taxis, mostly from
Des Moines, with one from Philly, along with a $240 cab fare
receipt, from when I missed the Super Chief in Omaha and
had to take a cab to Pierre, if I didn't want to lose the trail
of the guy from Braintree. Per diems for sixteen days' work
are expected upon receipt of bill. Started late afternoon on

a Tuesday, so I didn't charge for that day but did include a receipt from Candlegrasse's Hardware for flashlight used to poke around the wine cellar of that lady in Cleveland Heights. No charge for cartridges. I would have bought them anyway.

As for the weight of my report, thought it best for all concerned not to write it up, as it implicated you, nailed you, in fact, which, I must say, did not surprise me in the slightest. I have been in this racket long enough to know that half the time the one who hires you to solve a crime did it himself, though frankly I wonder why you went to the trouble to look me up in the first place. You could have saved us both a lot of time and green by confessing from the git-go, rather than waiting for me to catch you. Maybe you thought that if I didn't catch you, then you didn't do it. But I did. And you did.

So there I stood, inspecting myself in the full-length mirror at the tuxedo-rental shop on Fourteenth, getting my outfit for the senior prom. I had never worn a tux before. "Isn't this supposed to be black?" I asked the proprietor who smoked a stogie and spoke like a gangster. "Black is out of style," he said. The tux was cobalt blue with white trim on the lapels. At home, my brother asked to look in the box. "Isn't it supposed to be black?" he asked. "Black is out of style," I said.

On the night of the prom, I picked up Ginny's corsage at the Gramercy Park Florist, a gardenia. I felt that the other customers were staring at me. When Ginny opened her door, she seemed startled. "Black is out of style," I said matter-of-factly. She smiled but said nothing. I pinned on her gardenia, and off we went. The night was cool and I began to feel more comfortable, forgetting about my cobalt blue tux, until we arrived at school and entered the gym. "What the hell?" said Valente as soon as I appeared. "Why are you wearing that?" I told him why.

WHO COULD HELP but wonder what the Gramercy Park Florist thinks about the flowers that surround him in tall vases and ceramic bowls and pots? On tables. In planters. Behind the cold glass. Roses, hibiscus, phlox, gardenias. He dwells in the middle of a vast corsage. But what does the Gramercy Park Florist think when he looks around him? Does he follow his nose? Does he think of his lot as eternally beautiful, his temperature-regulated paradise? When he proffers sunflowers to others, does he think he is making the rest of the world golden and innocent and full of wonder, the way sunflowers can? Or would he rather be somewhere else? Is his lot like the soda jerks' behind the counter, who wouldn't eat a bite of ice cream if you paid them, and their tongues curling from a surfeit of bliss? If only he could toss away every goddam flower in the shop. Sell junk instead. Sell fish. At night he thinks of Charlie Chaplin in *City Lights* and of the blind girl in the flower shop, whom Charlie helps to make see again, so that she may love another.

LIVE LONG ENOUGH as a detective, and you begin to realize something about the senses. The two you think you would miss the most if they were lost—seeing and hearing—may be the most expendable. Both reveal wonders, to be sure. Sunsets and the Rach Three. But they also can get things entirely backward, plain wrong. "I can't believe my ears." "I can't believe my eyes." Touch, taste, and smell, on the other hand, rarely are ever doubted. You never hear someone exclaim, "I can't believe my fingers, my tongue, my nose," because you can believe those senses. They are tied to reality. I live to see and hear the world. You, too. Of course we do. But, in my business, I do not trust the world I see and hear. The world I smell, however, the world I touch, and taste, well, that's another kettle of fish. This a detective learns, if he lives long enough.

To be sure, age insists on changes, a lighter gray here, a darker blue there. More people sit in judgment of you. There is more condemnation, reconsidered opinions. You tend to speak with fewer friends, though with those few, once in a while, you talk your head off, or theirs. And that surprises you. But you also care less about all that, for there are other things to occupy your senses. These days, I walk slower and more carefully, like a pro athlete avoiding an expensive injury.

I study the stone steps and take them as if I were an oaf in the universe. I clop from planet to planet, side-stepping the rings and the moons.

In the skull of the sky, I hear a rattling. In the rosy shells on the beach, the hoots of owls. In the midst of some trivial transaction, my fingers run idly over the piano keys, and the bank teller with whom I deal sings "Beale Street Blues" by Bach. In the nonexistent churchyard in back of my house, a pregnant girl lies supine, her brown belly a Quonset hut between the markers. Once in a blue moon, I swing my chain and hurtle into the stadium, shouting war cries.

I'LL LET YOU in on an advantage in growing old. You begin to believe what you feel. It takes a number of years to do this, quite a number in fact, but one morning in the shower or running home during a snowstorm, anywhere, anytime, you find yourself muttering something you've said your whole life. Only earlier in your life, it sounded like a mere suspicion of a truth, available to continuous correction and revision, or total dismissal, and now, in older age, it feels like the truth itself. It is the truth. When you were shadowing yourself as a boy detective, you were never sure enough about your feelings to call them you. In older life, suddenly (not really) they are you. Sure enough.

This is how we get down to cases with ourselves, I

think—the wanderings of the mind that very slowly over the years coalesce into a system of belief. Intuition shows itself as faith. And after all the heavings and torments of the spirit, when you hated this and resented that, and felt you knew the reasons why, there was still, during all that seething time, a quiet wind of thought working through you that contradicted all that. Give yourself time, and that wind becomes the only thing you truly trust.

Most of what we call a philosophy of life when we are young are merely moods. Eventually the mind craves more, like a child at a puppet show (non-Platonic) who, however much he relishes the gestures of the arms and heads, soon wants to know who is working the puppets. Sixty years ago, when I walked these streets, I was all moods. No longer. I feel myself molting toward truth. The bitterness withers of its own accord. The moods, having contended among themselves, have settled upon a leader, a set of principles. I love. Therefore I walk. This, by the way, is the best time of life to write, when writing makes you happy. "We are happy," said Yeats, "when for everything inside us there is a corresponding something outside us." I love these streets. They love me back.

WITHOUT THE SMELL of fresh oranges; without the pickle brine; without the puke stench on the subway platform or the cold sweetness of the fruit stand; without the scent of warm beer, grilled cheese, coffee, gasoline in the parking garage, the lobby air, the elevator air; without the sweat on the bus, or the odor of chocolate emitting from a fancy candy store, or soap from a fancy soap store, or the horses, dog shit, herring, saltines; without the whiff of perfume squirted on a wrist in a department store; without the stink of the zoo; without all that every step of the way, where would we be, pal? Minnesota. That's where.

WHY DO I think of this now? It was after a high school party at a classmate's town house. The house was on East Seventeenth Street, one block from our school, yet my classmate was late every day. No one could understand it. He was short, fattish, unsure of himself. His mother was pleasant enough, like fruit. She seemed to have settled into her place in the world. His younger sister, the same. His father, a doctor, had his office on the ground floor of their house. Also short and fat, he was unkind to his son, always comparing him unfavorably to his more assertive, apparently self-assured friends, like me. He would say things in front of his son—"Why can't you be more like *him*?"—that made me uncomfortable. His son would stare up at him in a terrible bewilderment.

So, I think of the night of that party, after I had taken Ginny home and was walking back to my own home, around midnight. It was spring and Stuyvesant Park was dark, the leaves and the trees dark. And I walked past the house of the doctor and his wife and daughter and son, all of them backlit in the blazing window of the second-floor living room. They were cleaning the room, picking up glasses and plates, and putting things back as they were, after the only party my classmate ever gave, or ever would give, in high school.

AND, WITH NO connection, this: the blizzard of 1947, and six-year-old me snowbound in a snowsuit, looking like a moon walker, standing atop the buried cars around the park, jumping from roof to roof and thinking, one could make a tunnel in all this snow, many tunnels, a network of underground corridors, in the city of cold dreams. Why, man, the snow that winter was the height of the park gates. White, white. The white-capped birds. Life blanketed like memory. The whole night, white.

AS TO THE twin beds with the red roses on the headboards: One day my room was mine and then it wasn't. I was informed that from then on (I was seven) I would be sleeping in one of my parents' twin beds. My mother would be sleeping in the other. My father would occupy my baby brother Peter's room, and Peter would be in mine. Years passed (I was ten) before my parents shared their bedroom again, but little else until my father's last few years. A recollection of not being able to fall asleep in my father's bed, of making a pup tent of the duvet, and crawling under. A recollection of the light shadows sidling across the ceiling above my head, created by the headlights on the street nine stories below. A recollection of wanting answers to everything.

THE TROUBLE WITH trouble when you are young is that you have no words for it, and without words you cannot clarify it or objectify it, and without clarity or objectivity you're stunned. Stunned like a stuffed owl. Your eyes are glass, your feathers glued. Something is happening around you, a lot actually, and much of it involves you. But you cannot get ahold of it or move toward it for a closer look, because you lack the words, you see, you do not have the words. You cannot wheel around the trees. For a while, all I would envision in the streets I walked was my forfeited future. I strode into the past. There was something wrong, dead wrong. But no one gave me the words. Which, I suppose, is why I am what I am today, what I have made of myself. A man of letters.

Stumped, Mr. Spade? Another case, another book. Close the book. Book him. Feel the power of the quest as it rolls through us? Be my partner, I'll be yours. We'll get through it. We will move through our life alone and within sight of each other. And if one of us is killed, the other will bring the bitch to justice, will send her over, no matter what, because that is what a detective does when his partner is killed. That's what he does.

THE WIND LIFTS like a bedsheet flapped over dry grass in the backyard, in the days when laundry was hung out to dry on a line. It takes my breath away, then gives it back. I would give my right arm to know what my parents said to each other before the knife passed between them, and then, after the long years and Dad's three heart attacks, what they said to make peace. Well, maybe my left arm. Just below the elbow.

Even if I were to make an educated guess, I'd probably be light-years off the mark. Truth is a sly fox anyway. You can receive the right words in the right order, every last one, and still hear babble. I think the hedge schools in Ireland a hundred years ago had the right idea. Hide from the ones who don't want you to learn something, so that, though you never actually learn a thing, you feel as if you do because of the hiding. Sometimes, when the laundry was strung out like smiling teeth, I would press my forehead against the bark of an elm and listen to the sheets chatter.

That was in Chatham, or Westport, or Weston, before or after a Little League game in which I hit a triple or a single that I stretched into a double. Either that, or I struck out with the bases loaded. Looking.

A YOUNG WOMAN in a bright green ski vest, jeans, and, for some reason, riding boots sits weeping near the statue of William Seward in Madison Square Park. Her left arm is extended along the top of the bench while her right arm is crooked and covers her face the way people do in a room full of smoke, to shield herself from the gaze of passersby. I pass by, on the verge of asking her, "Are you OK?," while a blind man could see that she is anything but OK. Love. That's my guess. She has lost her love. She may be the woman I saw in Starbucks earlier in the evening, the one in conversation with the young man with the TODAY hat. Maybe they went horseback riding. Maybe they were together a while, and now they're apart. He broke up with her. The TODAY hat was not from the TV show after all. He'd had it made to order to express his carpe diem attitude toward love. Here for her TODAY, gone tomorrow. In any case, ought I to retrace my steps and ask her if she's OK? Once I asked her if she was OK, I then could tell her that everything will be OK. Why would I tell her that?

'SUP, WILLIAM SEWARD? His statue goes neglected in Madison Square Park. Sculpted by Randolph Rogers, it was unveiled in 1876. Seward, Lincoln's secretary of state, and a New York senator before that, not to mention his Alaska, which everyone does—mention Alaska. A quill pen is sculpted in his hand, signifying, one supposes, the signing of the purchase called "Seward's Folly." He was a worthy man, a prominent man, his "folly" notwithstanding. Yet it is the folly that withstands. And his statue.

When it was first presented to the public, a critic noted that while Seward the man was "all head and no legs," his statue "represents the statesman with unusual length." Seems that Rogers initially set out to make a statue of Lincoln himself, but ran out of money and at the last minute, switched to Seward. Poor Seward. No one could get things right about him.

A small coincidence: Directly across Twenty-third Street from Madison Square Park is the Flatiron Building, designed by Daniel H. Burnham. The structure was so tall, New Yorkers thought it would topple. They named it "Burnham's Folly." Folly faces folly. The word seems to have disappeared from the national lexicon, perhaps because the original ideas proved not so foolish after all. More likely, modern catastrophes are too big to be called mere follies. Vietnam was deemed no one's folly, as I recall.

Madison Square is guarded by statues and monuments, an eclectic bunch. Northeast of Seward a sky-high flagpole serves as a monument to soldiers who died in the First World War, the names of battles carved into the massive marble block at its base—Champagne, Marne, Vittorio, Veneto, Somme, Meuse, Argonne. On the north side of the park, near Madison Avenue, stands a statue of David Glasgow Far-

ragut, Admiral Farragut of the War of 1812, looming over a
semicircular white wall in which the figures of two goddesses
or spirits carved in relief are facing away from each other. In
the northwest corner rises Chester A. Arthur, posed like so
many statues of the turn of the century, suggesting that he
has just risen from his thronelike chair to make a speech. If
it is hard to understand what President Arthur is doing in
President Madison's park, it is more intriguing to account for
the prominence of Roscoe Conkling, at the southwest corner. Conkling was a mid-nineteenth-century New York con-
gressman, whom Lincoln had called "well-cultivated, young,
handsome, polite, and withal, a good listener." On the other
hand, the secretary of the navy, Gideon Welles, called Conkling an "egotistical coxcomb." And someone else noted that
he possessed "the finest torso in public life," causing one to
wonder how torsos were assessed in private life.

Some other statues in my world included the bronze Peter
Stuyvesant in front of St. Mark's Church in-the-Bowery on
Tenth Street and Second Avenue. His tomb lies in the church
basement. I saw it as a kid, staring and wondering about the
condition of the body and the peg leg. Was the peg intact?
In recent years, I've read that Stuyvesant was a prick and an
anti-Semite. But my mind still gloms on the peg.

In the center of Gramercy Park, green, bronze Edwin
Booth rises from his Hamlet's throne, superior to all that flesh
is heir to. He faces the National Arts Club and the Players

Club, on the south side of the park, which Booth founded in 1888. Whatever other purposes they serve, New York's statues are monuments to stillness, anomalies in the city. When I was in my teens I wrote a poem about the Booth statue, my first published piece, in the *Gramercy Graphic,* the neighborhood magazine. Something banal and too direct, about pride and adamantine shapes.

EDWIN BOOTH MAY have loved his brother with a special feeling, because being related to John Wilkes Booth allowed Edwin to play Hamlet with more oomph. He never said so in so many words (or in any words, far as I know), and he probably expressed shame at being related to Lincoln's assassin. But secretly he must have been grateful to brother John for informing Hamlet's ambiguities and vacillations. Can you love your brother, whom the world despises? To be or not to be. It was *Our American Cousin* playing at Ford's Theatre that dreadful night, everyone knows that. Would it not have been more interesting if *Hamlet* had been on the boards instead? Hamlet, starring Edwin Booth, the nation's greatest Shakesthespian, while John Wilkes was sweating, skulking in the wings? At the onset of which scene would the assassination have been most fitting? Not the soliloquies, surely. The swordplay near the end, perhaps. Or the graveyard scene, just as Edwin catches sight of his brother rushing the balcony, popping the president, and leaping, limping away. "Alas, I knew him," he says, examining his brother's skull.

You don't need to tell me: I am aware of how often I have summoned Lincoln to our walk. This is strange to me. I never have studied Lincoln, never have given him more thought than most people do. Once, though, I read his first inaugural address, I forget why, and when I had finished, I stood to catch my breath. How great was that man's soul. How strong his embrace of the meaning of the nation. And of us, the people. And our better angels.

IN EVERY DETECTIVE story there comes the moment when the body is discovered, sometimes just one body, and the pursuit of the murderer proceeds from there, sometimes two or three bodies, to deepen the mystery and ratchet up the fear. Whenever the police look upon the corpse, they are businesslike. Nothing tender or sympathetic is ever said, and this makes sense, because at that moment of discovery, the body is not a person but rather a puzzle. First they ask, how was he killed? In Philo Vance's *The Kennel Murder Case,* the despicable Archer Coe was done in three different ways, by dagger, bludgeon, and pistol. Vance solved the case by determining the stages at which Coe received each death blow. Only after people determine how the body was killed do they ask who dunnit, and why.

Occasionally, a murder story involves no body at all at first, just the announcement of a missing person, presumed dead. The body may appear eventually, as in *Chinatown,* where the mystery is established before the murder is revealed. But sooner or later, a body is a necessary feature of every murder mystery. It lies there, still, on the bed or on the floor, receiving, perhaps, more attention than it received in life. For the moment, beyond its last, it is the center of the universe. Nothing can move without it, though it has stopped moving itself.

But note the reactions to it. If a housemaid or another stranger or a relative comes upon the body first, that person screams. If it is the private eye who comes upon the body, there is no emotional reaction whatever. Detectives live in a world where dead bodies are to be expected. Death is life. Life is death. Yet if you listen carefully, you can hear a faint sigh of resignation and disappointment issue from his lips— before he calls the cops, before he goes to work solving the crime—as if to say, this is the way of the world, the sad way of the world.

If only he could have prevented the crime. If only he could prevent all the crimes. The word *Gramercy* comes not from anything grand or from "thanks" in French, or from "grant us mercy" in Shakespeare, but rather is a corruption of the Dutch *krom moersje,* the "crooked stream" that ran under the earth in downtown Manhattan, under everything, water

in the shape of a knife. Even now, if I tread carefully, I can feel
the water running under the world like the Kagera River in
Rwanda. I hear it, taste it. What is at stake in a detective story,
after all? It is the cry that runs under the earth and drives the
PI to do his duty. It is the cry for help, the insistent plea to
save some from others. Lives, reputations, happiness are at
stake. Time is pressing. Help! Do you hear something?

Fu-uh-uck! A shout out of nowhere preceded by a car
door slamming. City noise. Much is made of New York nightlife. Drunks. Louts. And the city that never sleeps because of
them. Little is made about the majority of citizens who sleep
the city nights away and dream of terrors from which they
are rescued in the morning. Their days are streaked with era-
sures. They suspect foul play but have no proof of it. Night
imagines night, which can be far more nerve-wracking than
actually experiencing it. You may think the nightlife of New
York is more exciting than the world of sleep, because that
is what you've been told by the Chamber of Commerce. But
beneath the flickering eyelids real tumult reigns. That's a fact,
Jack. Red Mars rises over Gramercy Park in the wintry sky.

    Those nights I lay alone in darkness in my parents' bed-
room—to recall them does not make me sad. Instead, I felt a
kind of safety, even though I was anything but safe; imperiled
is more like it. Still, I lay there like rags tossed on the cool

sheets, steeped in the liquid mercury of the sky over the park, still, quite still, and wracked with more wonder than sorrow. Do country kids feel the same way in their thick-wood country beds, big as sea turtles heavy with eggs, and their quilts and their cord of wood stacked in the driveway? I lay down in darkness in the city. Memory brings freedom, and freedom is always a blessing, no matter how it arrives. Sounds seep through the wall. My father soothes a patient on the phone. My brother whimpers.

PETER TOOK UP the trumpet at twelve, and a little later the piano. He was good at both, and I admired his discipline— how he learned to read music quickly and well. In my room with the door shut, I would listen to him practice—the dogged repetition of the scales—wondering what would become of him after I'd left the house forever. He knew that day would come, and that he would be alone with my parents and they with him. He was what kept them together and apart. They had no life without him, and he had no life with them.

When I was at Harvard, I wrote a long letter to my father imploring him to allow Peter to go to college outside New York. If Peter did not get away from that house, I told my father, he was doomed. My father wrote back a curt note, saying that my letter was "romantic" and that he knew best what my brother required. Peter wound up at NYU's School of Education, in a program for high school music teachers. Every night during his first year, he told me, he cried.

In the long run, he made better use of his talent. He got into the Mannes School, and later Juilliard, and he became the composer he had wanted to be from the beginning. He did all that on his own, with no real help from me. Had I been a better brother to him as we were growing up, I would have paid him more attention. But I deserted him, who should have been my partner. Detectives tend to dismiss their successes, but they live with their failed cases forever. In another room, my brother plays the scales on his trumpet, and I lie back with my arms behind my head like wings.

WHEN HE WAS fifteen, and I long gone from the house, Peter witnessed a fight between my parents in which my father broke a vase my mother had made in a ceramics class. The vase stood on a small table in the vestibule between the foyer and my parents' bedroom. It was green, with dark lines bleeding to the base. Peter said the lines looked like the hooves of horses. My father smashed the vase with his fist.

Around that time, Peter bought my mother the gift of a mandolin. She had not played one since she was a young woman. They played duets, my mother and Peter, with Peter at the piano—tunes he had written himself for the two of them—playing long into the afternoons.

YET THERE MY mother sits, harmless as Delft china at the dinette table, reading Emerson and Thoreau. In her mid-seventies, before Alzheimer's or the series of small strokes (the doctors were never certain which), she would teach Emerson and Thoreau to members of a community center on Fourteenth Street, called the Emanuel Brotherhood. She would laugh as she told me that her students would correct both authors at every turn, based on the experiences of their long lives. "He's got it all wrong," they would tell my mother.

Yet there my father sits in the red chair, reading Bruce Catton. How he loved reading about the Civil War, when he was not reading about the history of medicine. He published articles in a journal put out by Johns Hopkins on the history of medicine. He took a quiet pride in that, and in books he wrote on TB and cancer of the lung, to which he gave "the fault, dear Brutus" epigraph.

I wish only to remind myself that they were people, not just my parents. She in her housedress. He in his smoking jacket. Reading and writing in the vast apartment, and looking up from time to time to consider a fact, or an idea, or a memory. Even *they* had memories. Even *they* could have written a memoir. This I *shall* take from Dr. Johnson: "A wise man will make haste to forgive, because he knows the true value of time and will not suffer it to pass away in unnecessary pain."

OF HIS MADEMOISELLE, his nanny as he was growing up, Nabokov writes that he may have missed something essential in his long depiction of her. In his detailed descriptions of her vast size, her Frenchness, did he overlook those qualities that could have accorded her "a permanent soul," a place in eternity? In short, he wonders, did he salvage her from fiction?

It is one of the matters one worries about in doing a memoir. In class, we spend a lot of time kicking around the idea of memory—how accurate memory is, how selective, where it originates and why. However sketchlike the pictures I draw of my parents—have I salvaged them from fiction? In my mother's temerity, my father's crust, did I overlook the subtle motions of their minds, their troubled consciences? Detective work when applied to one's own family, perhaps especially then, is a bitch. There are too many temptations to follow false clues and rush to solutions. It is too easy to read crimes in mere errors or accidents. What am I recalling here on this walk, as I wander toward my beginnings? The agony of the timid woman, the self-doubt of the bull-headed man? Do I invent what I remember? Memory may be deformed into opinion, and be just as imperfect. I tell the story of my life, the story but not my life. Time is not to be believed in, for then you have to also believe in boundaries and categories as definitions of life. There is a connection between the memoir class I am teaching and this walk I am taking. I must remember what it is.

AND THERE YOU are, Dad, dying of congestive heart failure, which you tried to treat yourself, as I am flying back through the fog, on a winter night like this, trying to reach you. Officially, the El Al flight did not exist, since the plane was flying on a Saturday—no flights in Israel on Shabbat. I had arrived only the day before with a group of journalists invited to write about the country. At the airport, officials greeted me with the news of your dying. I spent the afternoon at the Wailing Wall doing my level best to pray, and the following morning I was off in the empty jet, trying to get back to you. I could not do it. New York was socked in. The fog was so thick, we had to land at Dulles and wait it out. I could not see past the window. Ginny and the children were with Mom and Peter. Peter answered the phone, and when he hesitated, I knew you were dead. In fact, I knew you were dead when I still was over the Atlantic, on my nonexistent flight.

And there you are, Dad, dead. And I am thirty-four, and sitting shiva with Peter and Mom, because Mom wanted the ceremony, with the mirrors covered with bedsheets and the dark apartment darker than ever. Mom's friends came, women with whom she had taught school so many years ago. And others from your old neighborhood. You would have cringed. Ginny had taken the kids home to Washington. I sank into the red upholstered chair as though a dense fluid were filling my body and weighing it down. A teacher friend of Mom's addressed me sympathetically. I looked so tired, she said. I started to answer her and fell asleep in midsentence. I must have spent that night in the apartment, but I cannot recall what room I slept in.

So LET US now praise Dad for taking me to *The Band Wagon* when I was twelve. We often went to movies together, just the two of us, while my mother stayed home with Peter. And *The Band Wagon* was playing in the neighborhood, at the Gramercy Cinema on Twenty-third near Lex. I am passing the place right now. Today the theater shows live music groups. Back then it showed Fred Astaire, Cyd Charisse, Oscar Levant, Nanette Fabray, and Jack Buchanan, an English music hall star who was wonderful in *The Band Wagon*. I could have watched that movie forever. I don't know why. The songs, perhaps, and a kind of sweet sadness to the story, though it ended well. It was a musical, after all. Maybe it was simply Fred Astaire, who, late in his career, seemed to swoop and glide over life like a melancholy tern.

The very next day, after school, I went over to the record store on Twenty-third, near Morton Stamps, but they only had *The Band Wagon* music on a 33⅓ rpm record, which my phonograph could not play. Yes, they could get me an album of 78s, but it would cost a fortune of $25. So I saved up. I clutched the album to my chest. At home, I played the set of records, everything in the movie, over and over. The triplets song, "Dancing in the Dark," "You and the Night and the Music," "I'll Go My Way by Myself," and "Oh, Give Me Something to Remember You By."

And let us praise him for a quiet sweetness that crept in from time to time, in spite of his efforts to keep it at bay. That nightly ritual, for instance, when he'd settle in his easy chair, a Scotch in hand, and watch *Perry Mason* reruns. For a detective like me, especially in my hypercritical teenage years, Perry Mason was clownish—those oversize people solving crimes in a courtroom, every suspect looking guilty but the killer. But Dad loved the neatness of the show. And I watched it with him, as if I liked it too.

And who can forget the time I told my parents I'd rather spend that Saturday wandering around the neighborhood alone than go for a ride with them and Peter, and after they had driven off, and I regretted rejecting their offer, Dad had circled the park to give me a chance to change my mind, which I did. That time. Or the time (where's the ledger?) I came upon a sparrow with a broken leg, lying on its side in a corner of the park. I brought it to my dad, whose office then was at number 45. It occupied the ground floor opposite another doctor, a man with a handlebar mustache who kept a talking parrot on a wooden perch on the sidewalk outside his office. I carried my sparrow inside, and my dad rigged a tiny splint. The bird looked surprised to be alive and to be wearing a splint. "What should we do now, Dad?" He said we should create a nestlike place on the sill outside my ninth-story window. When the sparrow felt strong enough it would fly, he said. One day, it did.

AND LET US now praise Peter, who could be funny when we needed it, who, when we were sitting in the professionally somber waiting room at the Frank E. Campbell funeral home on Madison, arranging for Dad's cremation, having just spoken with the professionally somber funeral director, glanced at the box of Kleenex on a table and said, "I'm surprised the Kleenex isn't black." And thoughtful. Some weeks ago he sent me a masterly charcoal drawing he'd made of Poe's raven, along with "The Black Cat," in *Pictorial National Library,* the original magazine in which it was published in 1848. A first edition of the story. He found it in New York's old Argosy Book Shop many years ago and bought it because he loves Poe. But he knows that I am a detective, and so he just decided to give it to me. The other day, I was startled to read, for the first time, Poe's poem "Alone": "Then in my childhood, in the dawn / Of a most stormy life—was drawn / From every depth of good and ill / The mystery which binds me still."

THERE IS A moment on a walk when you look away from something or someone you have been looking at, and then look back. The object appears farther away than when you first saw it. The act of looking away, of deliberately ignoring the object—or perhaps you were distracted, it makes no difference—the act of looking away seems to have distanced the object from you. The object has receded from your point of view. That bench over there in Union Square, for instance. I was walking straight toward it, when I averted my gaze for no more than a few seconds, and then returned it. Though the bench was actually closer to me, it appeared to have moved back a few yards. Nothing had happened to the bench, but something had happened to me. In the instant I looked away, I drifted and forgot where I was. I occupied a different place from Union Square, though I cannot say what. Perhaps I was dwelling in the past, or in the stars, so when I returned to the world in which I walk, everything seemed new and strange to me, almost alienated. We appear to be near things and to one another. Yet we are just as close to being far away.

LET ME SPEAK to you of three walkers—Rousseau, Hesse, and Bashō, especially of Bashō. All three made good use of walking, according to their different temperaments. Rousseau, the most analytical of the three, called his walk-thoughts "reveries," but they are more like sorrowful rants than to dreams. He took his long walks at the end of his life, and while he has a number of philosophical bulletins for the world that has rejected him, he thinks principally about himself, his self-imposed exile, smarting from every real and imagined persecution. Even as he searches for rest and calm, he seems incapable of avoiding the methodical. There is one nice moment. He calls himself a solitary wanderer but acknowledges that no one is truly solitary but God, to whom he ascribes complete solitude, thus complete happiness.

Less deliberate, Hesse called his account *Wandering*. His tone is far more serene: "The world has become lovelier," he says. "I am alone, and I don't suffer from my loneliness. I don't want life to be anything other than it is." Unlike Rousseau's forced march, there is nothing irritating about Hesse's sojourn, which is kept quiet by interspersed drawings and poems. Still, one gets the picture of his walking against the tide, an awareness that the calm he has achieved runs counter to his former self. And we can hear the din of that rejected world in the background.

But Bashō. Wonderful Bashō. The wanderer's wanderer. The pure observer, as he takes to *The Narrow Road to the Deep North*, in the Japanese provinces during the seventeenth century. Where Hesse insists on his enlightenment, Bashō is imbued with it. He perfected the haiku, which seems the ideal form for recording discrete moments of a walk. How lovely is this: "Breaking the silence / Of an ancient pond / A frog jumped into water / A deep resonance." Bashō said, "Go to the pine if you want to learn about the pine." A first-rate private eye, that Bashō.

AS WAS BLIND Hector Chevigny. When he came storming around the park, you'd better not leave your bike or skates in his way. He could wield that white stick like a scythe, and he seemed angry enough as it was without anyone doing anything to irritate him further. Neither his blindness nor his temper impressed me as much as his being a writer, and a mystery writer, to boot. He wrote scripts for the *Mr. and Mrs. North* series. We had actors aplenty in Gramercy Park. John Barrymore was said to have lived in number 36. Humphrey Bogart married Helen Menken in the Gramercy Park Hotel. John Garfield died in the sack in number 4. In my lifetime, there were John Carradine, and Royal Dano who played Lincoln, and Margaret Hamilton, whom younger kids approached with caution whenever she was sitting in the park, lest she let out the witch's cackle that made her famous in *The Wizard of Oz*. James Cagney lived in number 34 for a few years. I saw Charles Coburn once, stepping out of the Players Club, yet another Stanford White building. I waved. He waved.

But Mr. Chevigny, the mystery writer, was in a class by himself. He quick-stepped everywhere, as if on a furious mission, his own "Wizard," his German shepherd, at his side.

Often he walked too fast for the dog, which was why we kids had to be alert not to leave anything he could trip over in his path. His autobiography was an homage to Wizard. He called it *My Eyes Have a Cold Nose*.

One day, when I was thirteen or fourteen, he invited me to his apartment in number 34, where he lived with his wife, a kind and gracious woman, and his two gifted children, one of whom, Paul, became a writer, too. I do not know why he summoned me. Perhaps someone had told him I was a detective. I had no idea he knew I existed. We sat together in his study. It was my first time talking with a blind person, and I wasn't sure where to look. His ferocity had vanished, as he spoke of the special difficulty of writing for radio. "It's tricky," he told me, "especially hard to impart information, like exposition."

"How do you let an audience know something that one of the characters can't know?" I asked him.

He said, "Have one of them whisper to another."

One night I was listening to *The Shadow*. There was a moment when Lamont Cranston needed to inform the audience that some time had passed between scenes. Cranston said, "Well, Margot, here it is the next day."

23 PACES TO Baker Street. Have you seen it? Another movie about a blind detective, or rather about a blind playwright in London, who overhears a kidnapping plot and takes on the role of detective. Van Johnson as the writer, embittered because his blinding was sudden and recent, caught in the old predicament of knowing that a crime is to be committed with no one believing him, especially Scotland Yard. A murder is involved, and a couple of attempted murders. The movie appeared in 1956, when I was fifteen, past the years of my boy detective in the streets, and I had no creative outlet for my solitude. My family remained remote, my school a waste of time. I kept returning to *23 Paces to Baker Street.* There was much to glom onto in the story. Baker Street. The foggy atmosphere of London. The writer-detective from whom everything was taken, and what was not taken he cast away. Eventually he is proved right about the crime, of course. But until he abjures his bitterness, he is alone.

DOES A BLIND mystery writer feel his way into his work? Writing isn't science. Neither is most detective work. Explaining why he picked teams at random in a football pool, Chief Superintendent Foyle told his sergeant, "Science is not my strong suit," which is generally true of the trade. Exceptions are Patricia Cornwell's Kay Scarpetta novels, the TV show *Bones,* and the TV series *Quincy, M.E.,* about a forensic expert played by Jack Klugman. But most private ops operate by intuition and by knowing how people tick. Vance made a fetish of his understanding of character and personality. Others don't speak of it directly, yet it is clear to the reader that however many hard clues may lead to the guilty, it is character that does them in. To kill for envy, one must be capable of envy. To kill for passion, one must not necessarily be outwardly passionate, but rather have passion smoldering within. See Clifton Webb in *Laura*. Or Laird Cregar in *I Wake Up Screaming*.

And this capability to delve into the human psyche, however corrupt that psyche may be, accounts, I think, for the deep vicarious pleasure we take in a mystery story. Mysteries are like sports. Someone wins, someone loses. And that clean conclusion is always satisfying in anything. But the mystery story is better than a baseball game or a tennis match, or a football game, European or American, because there is always a tinge of ambiguity to be detected and relished—some trace of mixed feelings, or sympathy for the culprit, along with a deeper understanding of human nature as a result of the crime. The story told to us is more organized and more complete than our own lives. And it has an ending. A case is closed, unlike anything in reality. But before that door clicks shut, before justice prevails, we may dwell in the house of a mind other than our own and see into a human capability that we may, and must, deny ourselves.

Would you kill for money if you were assured of money, a great deal of money? Would you kill for revenge if you were assured of revenge—just, satisfying, delicious revenge? Advancement in business? Triumph in love? Would you kill for

such things if the mere act of killing would hand them to you
on a platter? Probably not. I do not know you that well, but
probably not. Still, is it not intensely pleasurable to watch
someone else act in your worst self's behalf, commit the crime
for you, as your surrogate, and then take the rap for you, too?
Better than that, as a reader, it was you who tracked yourself
down. It was you who made the fatal error, that slip of the
tongue, and it was you who caught it, and you who brought
yourself to justice. So now you may breathe two sighs of relief.
No football pool will give you all that.

YET WHY DID he do it? If that question is asked in a mystery
story, it usually comes after the crime has been solved and
the criminal is caught or dead. An innocent asks why he did
it. And the detective often says something vague and poetic.
After the Maltese falcon brings about a couple of murders, the
cops ask Sam Spade what the bird was. He could have said
"money," but his answer is Shakespearean—"the stuff that
dreams are made of."

That answer could apply to more stories than *The Maltese Falcon.* Only in the simplest mystery stories are motives
clear-cut. In *Double Indemnity,* why does an insurance agent
who has followed the straight and narrow all his life turn on
a dime and conspire with a beautiful woman to murder her
husband and get his money? Is his motive the money? The

woman? Or is it something unseen, unspoken of in the story itself—attached to the straight and narrow of the salesman's life, or to something buried way in his past? Or to nothing articulate? A motive may be untraceable yet still be a motive.

Ask the why-did-he-do-it question of the grease monkey in *The Postman Always Rings Twice* or of the hapless attorney in *Body Heat*. In both cases the men seem duped. They never murdered anyone until love and money combined to prompt them. The women, too, may serve as evil temptresses, but until the right wrong guy came along, no blood was on their hands either, as far as we know. If you think that sex and a fortune are enough to drive people to do the worst things in the world, you don't know much about the world. The lovers in all these stories could have walked away after second thoughts, but they didn't. Why did they do it?

For the detective, motive is no more or less important than any item of information leading to the crime's solution. Unless, as in *The Maltese Falcon*, he gets involved with the murderer herself, he couldn't care less about motive. And even in that story Spade had decided long ago that dreams, of love or money, make no killing excusable. I'm not even sure how much motive matters for the reader, since he too gets drawn toward the solution of the crime rather than the inner workings of the criminal. But in life outside detective stories, why does anyone do anything? Murder. Mass murder. I used to think that boredom, ennui, was the reason for most of the world's crimes, like wars. But boredom is merely the fallow field for that awful still silence in which our minds show themselves capable of anything. Hitler, for instance. Why did he do it?

ALL RIGHT, I'LL TALK. But you'll never take me alive. I've seen to that. My side of the story? You really want my side of the story? About my military skills? My ambitions to conquer Europe? About the Russia fuck-up? About my youth as a painter? I'm just yanking your chain. I know what you're after. *Why?* You really want to know? You won't like it. Oh, what am I thinking? You don't like anything about me. I bet you suppose it has something to do with their money, don't you? Well, for one thing, most of the ones I dealt with didn't have ten deutschmarks to their name, and those who did I admired. Having money means you stepped on someone to get it. I'm all for stepping on someone.

Or you think it was their clannishness, which, I'll admit, did get under my skin. (I know you don't want to hear about skin. Can't take a joke?) But I didn't really care if they kept to themselves. Fact is, the camps were logical extensions of their clannish behavior. Involuntary to be sure, but no one can say I didn't keep them together in one place or in several, until, of course. . . . But no, it wasn't the clannishness either. Or the hairdos. Or the hats. Or the language. Or any of the tools they used to shut the world out.

You really want to know why? Because they endured. That's why. Because, century after century, visionaries like myself have tried to wipe them from the face of the earth, and you've got to admit, I came close. The closest. No luck. The reason I tried at all is because Jews endure. Hate 'em, love 'em, ignore 'em, shoot 'em, they just walk on and on and on. Who could stand by and watch that happen? I ask you. Happy now?

SO NICE NOT to be going anywhere tonight. I could be on my way to my publisher, to promote myself in my appealing self-effacing way. I could be going to the supermarket, where I would chuck my assignment to buy aluminum foil and fresh peas and bananas, and pick up a fistful of Devil Dogs instead. I could be strolling over to my friend Garry's house, where we could figure out something to do, because long ago we concluded that life consists of something to do. I could be headed for the dermatologist so that she could tell me that the melanoma-looking stain on my left leg isn't melanoma after all, and she's shocked because she knows I go out in the sun without sunscreen, and she could frown. I could be going to the funeral of a former colleague at which I am to speak, rehearsing what I shall say so that it appears spontaneous. Or I might be going directly to the gravesite. But I am not going anywhere tonight.

Some use solitude like this productively, creatively. Many

of my writer friends hide away in far-off places to do their work. I do not make any such use of my solitude. In fact, I write more easily in the company of others, when my family is in the house and I can sense their warming presence in distant rooms. When I am alone, I usually just sit around watching sports or movies on TV, or take a walk, as I am doing now, feeling more like myself than I do with people. Aloneness is my place in the world. It no more pleases or displeases me than my skin.

The solitude of city walking is different from the kind that mountains give you or the sight of violet trees in the fall. City solitude does not befall you like a blessing, does not insinuate itself. You earn it. Instead of shutting out the noise of the people around you, you embrace all the noises on your cluttered walk, remaking solitude into multitude. How to walk in the world? Surely, that question is not mine alone. Everywhere is within walking distance.

A backcourt man at the University of Arkansas, a playmaker, was going through a cold spell. He couldn't shoot. His passes missed their targets. He asked his coach what he thought was going wrong. The coach told him to get a friend to take a stopwatch and time exactly how many minutes and seconds the player had his hands on the basketball during a game. The player was astonished to report that in a regulation forty-minute game, he had touched the ball only slightly over two minutes, the discovery being all the more surprising since, as a point guard, he would have his hands on the ball more than his teammates would. "So what do you learn from this?" asked the coach. The kid shrugged. "You learn that most of the game is played away from the ball." I am a very small part of these streets.

THIS IS TWENTY-SIXTH and Madison, the site of New York Life, where a depot stood in the 1860s, until P. T. Barnum turned it into Barnum's Monster Classical and Geological Hippodrome. It was renamed Gilmore's Garden in 1876. William Henry Vanderbilt renamed it once again as Madison Square Garden and opened it for cycling. Stanford White (he got around) designed the second Madison Square Garden, which opened at the same location in the 1890s and was torn down in the early 1920s. A new one was erected on the West Side in 1925, and there have been two more Madison Square Gardens since, neither of them near Madison Square.

What New York kid reared on basketball did not dream of playing in Madison Square Garden? In the vast echoic place that smelled of sweat and hot dogs, my high school friends and I watched the great pro players like Bob Cousy and Paul Arizin, and the great college players like Bill Russell and Jerry West and Oscar, each of us bouncing in the cheap seats high above the court, dreaming ourselves into every pass and shot, locked in our private tales of triumph. I can recall few pleasures equal to the flick of the wrist and the lowering arm and the ball arcing toward the basket. At its best, it was like writing at certain mystical moments. You didn't plan it. You didn't think about it. You jumped and let the right word fly into the hole. All net.

And then, all of us loping downtown toward home and shouting to one another as we relived the game. This pass. That shot. The cold mist of our breath. The fires of memory. Air-passing and pantomime dribbling around and shooting over the heads of the grim grown-ups on the street and the scowling cops.

I'D LIKE TO go back to your life statement, if I may.

I thought we were finished, Lieutenant.

Almost. You said you never bothered to learn how to do things the right way.

Well, not the way they're supposed to be done, anyway.

Whatever. You sound . . . and I went over my notes to make sure I got it right. You sound as if you have lived impressionistically.

Impressionistically. Yes. I think you could say that.

But aren't you concerned that by so doing, you've missed a lot? I wonder if you think the Impressionist painters missed a lot, too. Or, do you think they would say it was others who missed a lot?

Everyone misses something. The trouble with us impressionists is that we don't know we're impressionists. We think
we're realists.

That's messed up.

"Journey of life like feather in stream. Must continue with
current."

Bashō?

Charlie Chan. *In Egypt.* Can I go now?

One more question. Why did you become a detective?

To punish the guilty and rescue the innocent.

And did you accomplish these things?

Sure. Of course I did. You bet.

IF YOU LIVE like an impressionist, there's no carrying things
too far. When I wasn't occupied with a case as a kid, I spent a
good deal of time in Miller's and Kauffman's, examining bri-
dles, bits, crops, and saddles for my horse. The fact that I did
not have a horse never affected my enthusiasm for window-
shopping for equipment for which I had no use and I couldn't
afford anyway. Looking back, I'm not sure what I was doing
in the saddlery shops, but I must have had the impression that
I owned a horse or soon would own one. If ever a salesperson
in Miller's or Kauffman's approached to ask if I needed help,
I said no thanks.

IMAGINE WHAT YOU know. Shelley said something close to that in his *Defense of Poetry,* and I have appropriated the idea in my memoir course. In the early classes, I talked about the difference between invention and the imagination—the difference between, say, inventing a horse that merely talks, like Mr. Ed, and creating a horse that has something to say, like Swift's Houyhnhnms that bear the burdens of civilization. The imagination has different levels. You can imagine something that has never been seen before. And you can imagine something that has always been seen, yet never in the way you see it. For that you need to dream into the object of your attention, to see the inherent nobility in the animal that has borne so much without complaint and to make that animal ruler of the universe. Imagine what you know, I tell my students, and what you know will become wonderfully strange, and it will be all yours. More truly and more strange.

To push this idea along, I give them short exercises for their dreaming. The first day of class, I brought in a pair of old sneakers, running shoes, tossed them in the middle of the seminar table, and asked the students to imagine the ordinary sneakers before them. One young woman produced a piece about a man in the apartment across from her, who left one sneaker in the hallway outside his door every morning, because he had but one leg, and he needed that one sneaker, and then he put two sneakers out at night, as if to indicate that the other leg existed. In another exercise, I asked them to listen to a piece of music and to write a piece on what the music inspired. Poetry, fiction, memoir, anything. I did the same for a painting. And for a flower: Dream into a tulip. I asked them to write a piece from the point of view of a part of the body, and another from the point of view of a punctuation mark. You're a semico-lon, a hyphen. I asked them to write a piece from the point of view of a machine, to dream into the machine. The students became a bathroom scale, two clocks, an iPad, several cars, a guillotine, a vibrator, and a tattoo needle that spoke in rapid stutters. More dreams. I eat their dreams like candy.

LAST NIGHT I dreamed I was in my grandparents' tenement apartment at the corner of Ninth Street and Second Avenue, where I am standing now. Only in my dream the apartment did not consist of three smallish rooms, with a view of the sooty shaft that dropped to a dark pit three stories below. This dreamed-of apartment was a network, more like a maze, of some twenty rooms and five or six bathrooms. And I was trying to shave and get dressed so that I could join my friends, many of them, who were also in the apartment. We all were about to travel somewhere, and there was much hurrying-up and preparatory activity before we got under way. But I could not find my two suitcases, and I could not find my clothes. And by the time I did, and shaved, and prepared to join the

others, most of the people were already out the door. "Patta,"
I said when I ran into my grandfather at the dream's end. "I
did not remember that your place was so big." "Oh yes," he
said. "It has always been very big."

How long before I return to the monuments of my former yearning and feel nothing? Now, on Twelfth Street and
Second Avenue, I pass the Village East Cinema, which was
the Stuyvesant Movie Theater when I was a kid. Past where
the Jade Mountain Chinese restaurant stood until a few years
ago, where my family got takeout nearly every Sunday. I tired
of the routine. Peter tells me that one Sunday I finally balked
and told my parents, "I don't want to go to the Jade Mountain
or any other mountain."

Tonight I inspect the doorway to my grandparents' tenement at 148 Second Avenue in the gentrified neighborhood.
The building looks the same—same wooden doorframe,
same floral tiles on the floor. No matter how poor the residents all those years ago, there always were architectural gestures toward beauty. One thing is different. Where the names
listed in the hall register inside the front door were SPRUCH,
FINEBERG, COHEN, and GALLUZZI, now they are BEARDSLEY,
DAVIS, SHELLEY, and RIGBY.

One block farther south on St. Marks Place itself, I look
up at the six-story sand-color building, with the oval windows
and elaborate stonework near the roof, to the floor where
W. H. Auden had lived. At least, I always believed he'd lived

there. Not sure where I got the idea. But in my teenage years I would walk over to St. Marks Place from home or school, two or three times a week, and stand staring at the window I imagined to be his. I had read that he lived close to here—after a stint in Brooklyn Heights, where he shared a house with Carson McCullers and Benjamin Britten, and that he was a member of the St. Mark's Church in-the-Bowery congregation. I look up again tonight and reel in the stars.

Another resident of Auden's Brooklyn Heights house was Gypsy Rose Lee, who was known to most people for her principal profession. I knew nothing of that. Gypsy Rose Lee was known to me as the author of two mysteries, *Mother Finds a Body* and *The G-String Murders,* whose title ought to have given me a clue.

YEARS LATER, WHEN I was teaching writing at Harvard, I finally met Auden, which turned out to be a mistake. Occupying the lowest rung of the faculty ladder, I did all the scut work required by the English Department, such as ferrying notable visitors from receptions to readings and everywhere else. Auden visited, and I was to pick him up at Logan Airport. I hardly saw my assignment as scut work, not at first, and I drove through a snowstorm, like the one in his elegy to Yeats, to meet his plane.

Before I had left for the airport, a student from the *Crim-*

son, the Harvard newspaper, had asked me if he could have an interview with the great poet. I told him I'd try. When Auden descended the steps of the plane, in his bedroom slippers, into the snow, and we were walking to my car, I put in the student's request. "No interviews!" Auden said, which was the only thing he said until we arrived at the Faculty Club, where he was to meet the senior English Department members for lunch. The kid from the *Crimson* came toward us, pen and pad in hand, and I started to explain Auden's "no interviews" policy, when the poet waved me aside with a sweep of his arm. "Why, of course I'll talk to this nice young man," he said, as I, the horse's ass, retreated.

That night, he was shit-faced as well as sour-pussed. And, after a day of driving him here and there in the snow, Marianne Moore, or Richard Wilbur, or Robert Lowell, or anyone else who came to mind usurped him at once as my favorite modern poet. Come midnight, I was returning him to his Cambridge hotel in a near blizzard when, now stewed to the gills, he decided it would be a good idea to exit the car as I was going ten, maybe fifteen, miles per hour. So he opened his door to get out. Only a lingering respect for literature prevented me from letting him do it.

LITERATURE GETS ON your nerves, but you can't shake it. I was the world in which I walked. I am a little world made cunningly, said Donne. Yes, sure, as long as we concede that we are mysteries to ourselves, crimes never to be solved. Then the self-satisfied or microcosmic view means only that we are no more or less out of our reach than life itself. Keats relished dwelling in the mystery. Poe feared it. Emily Dickinson, not a bad PI herself, cautioned the surgeon that under his careful knife lies the culprit, life.

A man I met, so brilliant in math he made himself one of the richest fortunes in the world. All who spoke of him were excited with awe and amazement. He had solved a math mystery. Einstein and Darwin solved mysteries. Mystery. That's all there is. There is us. There is the knife. There is life, which is no walk in the park, you know. Or a day at the beach, for that matter.

IN A DINER on Thirty-eighth and Lex, the waitress approaches. Hair in a bun. Through-the-mill eyes. Am I ready to hear today's specials? No, thank you. Not quite yet. In an hour. A week at the outs. It is not that I don't want to hear today's specials. I just don't want to hear them now. You understand. So important is the business of hearing today's specials that I do not wish to rush into it. And, after all, hearing today's specials is only the beginning of the process. Once I hear today's specials, I will have to choose among them. And, for every special chosen, how many remain unchosen? Do the unchosen of today's specials feel less special for that? Are they consigned to a lesser menu, one that lists today's nonspecials, the ordinary average offerings of today? Am I afraid to choose? you ask. Not at all. I shall be happy with my special, once I make the choice. But I am not the only one involved in the transaction. Until I choose my special, no other special on the menu needs feel slighted. All specials will feel special, as they do now, which befits their designation as today's specials. And no special's self-esteem shall be diminished. And all shall be equally special in the eyes of the god of menus. All shall be free. So, you see, that is why I am not ready to hear today's specials. Not yet. In a year or so. Perhaps. My waitress gives me the once-over. If looks could kill.

WOMEN MAKE EXCELLENT killers in detective fiction because they catch you off guard, because, whatever you say, you don't expect the killer to be a woman. The reader takes his eyes off the woman as suspect, as in *The Maltese Falcon,* where all logic points to Brigid O'Shaugnessy from the start. Mystery writers count on that. In the third *Thin Man* movie, about a warring wealthy family on Long Island, the killer, Virginia Grey, was not only female, but she was also the daughter of one of the men she bumped off. And Agatha Christie had at least two guilty women in her canon, who killed for love or revenge. Passion more than personal gain comes into play when a woman does it. In most cases, you feel that a woman would not waste her time committing murder for money, and even when she does, as in *Double Indemnity* and *Body Heat,* there's always a man to go with the stash. But slight a woman or betray her or humiliate her or keep her down, and you'd better have eyes in back of your head.

What would it be like to be a woman, I wonder, a wonder woman, and know everything and say nothing? Men are given an easier time of it, maybe because we die first. So little to do, comparatively. But to be *her,* for instance, in the puffy pink coat and the cap with the teddy bear ears. Or *her* as she emerges from D'Agostino, angling her hip to accommodate her two-year-old, who can walk perfectly well on his own two legs but chooses not to. To be that woman who carries someone around unnecessarily, and who was built to do just that? Yes. That one. Another waking dream.

WAKING DREAMS. SHANK wrote of waking dreams. Subhumans invaded his loft here on Thirty-sixth Street between Fifth and Sixth. They stole a lamp and a vase, and took a shit on his bed. He told me about this with a kind of sad wonder one day when I visited him. The building that contained his loft stood next to Lord & Taylor's. It is gone, and so is Shank, but not from me, never from me. Jon Beck Shank succeeded Mr. Wilcox as our high school English teacher—the second and last creative light in the dead air of that school—and as my mentor in the detective trade. A poet, he wrote his one book, called simply *Poems,* while he was in the army. He, too, was fired by the school—not for being gay, though they gladly would have done it for that reason, but rather because Shank had standards. Parents complained to the principal when their kids, all of whom had been persuaded that they were geniuses, got Cs and Ds.

Here was a school whose Quaker educational vision allowed for the admission of one black student, just one, in the mid 1950s, and whose faculty included several outspoken anti-Semites, a couple of floozies, a leering pedophile who used to loiter around the boys locker room, at least two alcoholics who came to work with booze on their breath, a French teacher who spread rumors about the students, and a biology teacher who taught us that if a fat woman married a thin man, they would have an ordinary-size child. This was the place that fired Shank.

He would give our class Canada mints and ask us to write what the mint tasted like, to show us how to think in metaphors and similes. He would remove a key word from a line of poetry and tell us to fill in the blank, to see if we could figure out how the poet arrived at the right word. In Eliot's "Sweeney Erect," why does the poet use "suds" to describe Sweeney's face while he shaves? Sweeney, the comic-deadly, beer-drinking lecher. Why not "soap" or "foam"? Because they don't give us everything about Sweeney the way "suds" does. During this exercise, he would also ask us to pause to appreciate the beauty of the blank space, what discoveries it invited. When we studied *Hamlet* with him, he had us build an exact model of the Globe Theatre. Then we put on the play.

Flamboyant, six-foot-one or more, handsome in the way of Franchot Tone, he strode around the school wearing lavender shirts and crimson neckties. "My name is Mr. Shank," he announced at our very first view of him. "That's what you'll call me in class. What you call me outside of class is your own business." Wit? In that school? And more than witty—attentive, kind, generous. He gave our class books at graduation, each individually appropriate. Me he gave his book.

He had come to us from the Yale School of Drama, and before that from Brigham Young. He was the first Mormon any of us ever knew. Long after his dismissal, he died blind, from AIDS, I think. Long before that he had written: "People themselves glow in the glass air, slowly / Donning the lucent word as an incandescent sheath / Their waking dreams are become self-resolutions of strength."

NEVER HAD MUCH strength myself, unless an absence of fear counts as strength. I recall self-generated fear as a child when I would absorb the story I was reading or the movie I was seeing. But I cannot remember actually being afraid too often. Writing in war zones, I was made afraid not in Sudan or Beirut or even Rwanda—places where fear was both reasonable and rife. Fear made people crazy. During the Israeli bombing of Beirut in 1982, I was sitting in the lobby of the Hotel Continental. The swimming pool outside was empty. When a car bomb went off, a man panicked and jumped in the empty pool, breaking his leg. Just then, another man jumped in to rescue him, breaking his wrist.

In Belfast, however, I felt a fear so deep it froze me like Emily Dickinson's snake. And it was born not of bombings or shootings, but rather of the hatred in the air, colder than the day is now, by which one knew how dark the soul could turn. Without any demonstrable cause, you feared for your life.

Surprise, the element of surprise, can make you fearful in a mystery story—an act of violence in an unexpected place. In *Psycho,* the most terrifying moment occurs neither in the shower scene, nor at the ending when Mrs. Bates slowly turns toward us, but rather when the detective, Martin Balsam, mounts the stairs in the Bates house, and bewigged Norman, Anthony Perkins, rushes toward him with a knife and stabs him in the head. A scene in an underrated film noir, *The Dark Corner,* starring the unlikely pair of Mark Stevens and Lucille Ball, achieves the same effect. Clifton Webb, who had hired William Bendix to do a killing, now must get rid of Bendix. In the hallway of an office building, he maneuvers Bendix so that his back is to an open window. Then he pokes him with his walking stick and out goes Bendix, backward. Something about the aristocratic Clifton Webb doing in the big and brutal William Bendix so softly, with a walking stick. So quickly. Just like that.

JUST LIKE *THIS*, on Thirtieth between Park and Madison. What gets me is the speed with which he snatched her purse—faster than a cuttlefish's tongue (if it is a tongue), presto stealo, now you see it now you don't. The woman, caramel tan, well heeled, and sharp as the black leather purse taken from her, stands still, impressed. She cannot speak, much less scream. She stares after the thief, as if she were about to applaud. The thief, meanwhile, has long disappeared, leaving no trace of himself, like the moon. She smiles like an oyster. Well, can you beat that! she seems to say. And no one can.

LIKE MOST DETECTIVES, I occasionally turned to crime myself, thanks to Tom Brownell, the son of the future attorney general of the United States, under Dwight David Eisenhower. Tom taught me how to shoplift. "It's easy," he said. "Watch me"—as he sauntered into the soda fountain drugstore on the corner of Twentieth and Park, where my dad and I used to go, and swiped a fistful of candy bars. I took just one, but I was never as adept as Tom. The idea was to start with candy and work your way up to the costlier stuff, but I never made the grade, not even with candy. The Fifth Avenue candy bar I stole quavered like the *Hindenburg* over my bed that night. The following morning, I returned to the drugstore, and when the owner's head was turned, I restored the Fifth Avenue candy bar to its place on the rack, though I knew it was too late to restoreth my soul.

Sometimes Tom and I would play at his house after school. Tom's was a big dirty-white town house on what was called "the block beautiful"—Nineteenth Street between Third Avenue and Irving Place. Ted Husing, a radio sports announcer, had a house there with two black stone jockeys out front, which he painted white in the mid-1950s, to avoid giving offense, I guess. A movie star lived on the block, too, though I did not know her name. Tom's home, grand and bare, was cold in winter and also in summer. Upon entering after school, he went straight to his daily chore of collecting the dead mice from the traps and flushing them down the toilet. Then we could play.

In the winter of 1952, not long after the presidential election, cabinet appointments were announced. I went over to the block beautiful to see Tom. As I rounded the corner, his family was getting into a big black car. I waved, but Tom didn't notice me. That was the last time I saw Tom Brownell, the son of the future attorney general of the United States, under Dwight David Eisenhower.

EVERYONE ELSE SEEMED to belong to something—a club, a group, an institution. Tom Brownell used to show up in school once a week wearing the quasi military dress uniform of the Knickerbocker Grays. I never figured out what the Knickerbocker Grays did, but it seemed to involve marching and other martial exercises. Tom Munnell, the best student in our class, and the most gentlemanly, took figure-skating lessons in the afternoons. In the summers, he was a competitive sailor in Connecticut, winning races that were reported in the *New York Times* Sports section. He never mentioned his accomplishments. Some kids belonged to synagogues, some to churches. The one group I joined was the Cub Scouts, which met once a week in the basement of St. George's Church on Sixteenth Street and Rutherford Place. I remember only the blue uniform and the neckwear held together by a wooden clasp, and reading the Scout manual that taught you how to make a fire without a fire.

We walk through so many different lives, they say, a few of them ours. I don't buy it. Oh, we do different things, even look differently and think differently as we do them. But that is not the same thing as leading different lives. A principle persists in us, among all the changes—sometimes lived up to, sometimes denied. The deviations run their course. But eventually we settle upon who we are. Luke Appling, the once great shortstop for the Chicago White Sox, participating in an Old Timers game, hit a 360-foot home run into left center, at the age of seventy-five. That's who he was.

Who knows who *you* are? At the checkpoint, I demanded to see your papers. You blithely presented them as though you had done that a million times before. Such casual self-confidence. Such chutzpah. Driver's license. Birth certificate. Amex card. That should do it, you said. But I'm afraid there's been a mix-up (I'm trying to be polite). The name on your health insurance is not the name on your letter of recommendation, which, I may add, bears an illegible signature. And what you report as your blood type on your electric bill does not gibe with the character flaw noted on your passport. Would you mind stepping out of the line for a moment while we determine your IQ? It will only take a year or so, and then you can move along to Customs—whoever you are. Could you give me your name once more, for the record, but this time without the Lithuanian accent and the incessant shouting? Dimly, behind the steppes, the rising sun beckons you to originality. You. That's right—Mister Whatever You Call Yourself.

NOTHING PREPARES ME for this wind that comes in sideways at the corner of Twentieth and Third, flinging nails of ice and snow, and gulping and spitting in spurts so cold, you feel your eyes freeze in their tears. I cannot breathe. The owl, for all his feathers, is a-cold. It is as if this wind is telling me I have come to the end of everything, that there will be no going forward from this corner, no red sun in the offing, no flowers in bloom, only this shocking cold wall of air, from now on. The weight of it. If it could howl, I'd be deaf.

And then, just as suddenly, it loosens its hold on me, like a lion distracted by a noise in the brush, and it veers away, as if it never had been interested in me in the first place, as if, at this corner, I just happened to be in the wrong place at the wrong time. One moment I am clamping down on my teeth. The next, I stand confused. Did I dream the wind? Was its attack on me an accident? I think not. I sensed malice. In my hand lies a Stone Age ax, blood on the blade.

HAVE I TOLD you about the Case of the Decapitated Tulips? What am I saying? I know I haven't. Fact is, I haven't mentioned the case to anyone until now, because it happened to be one of those perfect crimes in which no one but the criminal knows who dunnit. I'm not even sure why I'm telling you about it now, because statutes of limitations do not apply to cases like this. Maybe I should keep my mouth shut. The perp is still at large. See if you can figure it out.

It happened in the spring when I was ten, just after the annual Gramercy Park Flower Show at the National Arts Club. One afternoon in early May, as was the custom, the neighborhood kids were drafted into helping out at the show, which consisted of a lavish display of flowers and a sit-down lunch for, mostly, ladies in bright hats with wide brims. The ladies ordered us about this way and that as we served trays of olives with the pits removed, pears with the skins removed, and sandwiches with the crusts removed, containing cucumbers with the rinds removed. There was no hardship in the work, except the irritating feeling of participating, and being shoved around, in a pointless ritual. After the event, the ladies thanked us perfunctorily, and the kids went home. Everything seemed in order.

But the following morning—and no one ever linked the Flower Show or the Arts Club to the crime—when the Gramercy Park attendants came to work, they discovered that every tulip in the park had been beheaded. The flowers, fifty or so, had been planted in neat rows in a large rectangular flower bed near the statue of Edwin Booth. Now their fallen heads—pink, yellow, white, and red—lay at the bases of the stems. It was horrible to behold, a massacre, reported the park attendants, those beautiful little tulips lying dead. Who would do such a thing? Most likely, the criminal acted alone. A gang of any size would have been noticed in the park on a spring evening at dusk. Someone from outside the neighborhood, "a troubled youth," probably. He must have climbed the gate, since it was unthinkable that anyone who lived on the park and possessed a key "would perpetrate an act of such wanton vandalism." And yet there were jagged cuts in the stems, which possibly could have been made by a key swung at the end of a chain. To this day, the case remains open. Solved it yet?

NOT TO MENTION THIS, not to mention that. Not to mention Joanna Miles's diary, which was on her bookshelf one time when she wasn't in her room, so I opened it and read it as any detective would. When she caught me in the act (she was a woman of eleven, I a boy of the same age), she told me in no uncertain terms, that PEOPLE DO NOT READ OTHER PEOPLE'S DIARIES. I should have known better. I probably did, though I don't think I'd ever seen a diary before or known anyone who kept one. Joanna was very sophisticated. She grew up to be quite a good actress. I used to love to go horseback riding with her and her friends in Forest Hills. But after that rainy afternoon, either she banished me from her house or I banished myself out of shame and embarrassment, and lost her friendship.

Hers was the oldest apartment house in New York, the very first one built, in 1870. It consisted of five floors, no elevator of course, with two apartments per floor, and in the center, a grand staircase with a brass railing that could have come from a European palace. (When Richard Widmark pushed the old lady in the wheelchair down the stairs in *Kiss of Death,* those were the stairs.) Dormers stuck out of a shingled mansard roof. And each apartment had seven large rooms and four fireplaces. Dark wood walls and wall sconces with converted gaslights. One day in the 1960s, a gang of dimwitted official hit men casually tore the building down, replacing it with a cheap-looking white brick apartment house. Nothing about it spoke of beauty, or of secrets.

NOT TO MENTION the slow raising of the barrel, as Dr. Donaldson, a crony of my father's, told me to lead the grackle and fire ahead of it, accounting for its flight path. "Wait. Wait." Not to mention the cold lawn of Dr. Donaldson's house in Smithtown, Long Island, and the brown leaves fallen. Not to mention the words of approval and encouragement as I squeezed the trigger, as instructed. Or the dead glass eye of the bird lying on its side, or the bellyache of helpless stupidity at the shower of congratulations.

FOR THE RECORD, let me state unequivocally that winter is a poor season for self-recrimination. The dead leaves lie sodden at the roots of the trees, and the roots look sallow, and the air is perturbed by an imaginable ice storm, and it's all wrong, the atmosphere, all wrong. There's no enchantment in it. Spring would make a better time. Bright summer, better still. Yet it can't be helped. It's winter. Make the worst of it.

On the other hand, let me also say, on behalf of winter, that it is quite a good season for horses. They stand in the hardened fields with their blank, dark eyes, still as boulders, and they see everything. They may appear to be idle or asleep, dying even, but they see everything. I liken myself and all PIs to the eye of the horse. Just wanted to state that for the record.

REDEMPTION IS HORSESHIT anyway. The nails in Jesus's hands. Redeemed in that? The efficient cruelty of tyrants? Is that redeemed by prayer? By conversion? By apologies? Look at the one in need before you, right now. Tend to her wounds. Or wipe the raspberry ice cream from her chin. Or give her a fresh pink tulip. Perk up. It is all the redemption a life requires. Of course, if you don't believe me, you can always spend your life on your knees, hoping you'll be noticed. People do.

A man I knew once, when he wasn't passing his days in church or praising Jesus, was occupied betraying others. Since he would tell them he betrayed them, he thought himself redeemed. Even now, fully forty years later, I see his face in its practiced innocence, sitting across from me at lunch, cleansing his little soul as he explained why he betrayed me. He felt better after that. I bleed in you. You bleed in me.

Oh well. We're all entitled to a few million mistakes. The vacant lot on Twenty-second and Lex, and the gang from Little Italy, rock-hard, pale, spectral, hurling chips of bricks at the tent we had pitched, and me running like crazy to escape, to fetch Mrs. Morris, too, but mainly to escape with my coward's heart intact. That definitely was in there, somewhere. Not to mention that, either.

One student asked, "What do these exercises have to do with our memoirs?" I told her, anyone can write a memoir about the events of a life. To do something originally yours, you must write about the dreams of your life, which are best disclosed in things you already know. "Is a memory a dream?" she asked. I don't know, I said. Most of them feel like a dream. "So many moments in a life," said another. "Yet life seems like just one moment," said a third.

AND YOU? *Toi?* Hold your breath, feel the balance of the barrel, lead the target, and squeeze the trigger. Everyone around you will die. And the world will bring you a report. Would it not feel better to hold your breath and stand there empty-handed? No gun or key chain. Who can ever get over the Rach Three—how he held all those instruments in his head all at once? You never know what is moving in your heart. The grackle in my sights no longer stirs, he of the still feathers and the stone eye. Sorry. You are not forgiven.

And yet were you not the one who ran toward the sea and spat back the salt and flipped your hair, peering through the droplets, through your own exploding breath, into the dark box? Remember him? Sure you do. The one who lay on his back on the fifty-yard line of the football field and swirled the stars? The one, there, standing head high in the light of the world? The one who spoke the truth? That, too, was you.

If you hope to improve your soul, you need to engage in self-destructive acts. Small ones, at first, until you get the hang of it—choosing the job that is wrong for you, or the town that is wrong for you. Once you are comfortable with those choices, you may move on and up to the wrong friends and lovers and mates, whose natures assure you of ruin. Then finally, there is you—your own worst acts and motives that gnaw at your skin in the sleepless nights, till you would cry out in the agony you have brought upon yourself. In these moments, you will feel a quiet heaving in your chest, and you will hear a voice very much like your own, telling you to "Wait. Wait." Then wonder about those you hardly know. Then wonder about those you will never meet. That is your improved soul.

A HORSE I rode in Forest Hills, a chestnut named Prince, tried to crush my leg against a wall as we participated in a ceremony for the opening of an indoor ring. I didn't take it personally. He wanted to get me off his back. A reasonable ambition. But I had to show him who was boss, so every time he sidled up to the wall, edging his flank closer, I hit him with my crop and dug in my spurs, yanking his bit to tear at the sides of his mouth, so that he, too, would feel pain. This is how it went with us, beating each other up, riding in a circle of show horses, other riders carrying flags, he hating the ceremony he was forced to participate in, I hating it, too.

Would anyone really mind if I rode Prince through my old neighborhood at night at a full gallop, squeezing his barrel ribs with my thighs, nudging his belly with my silver spurs, belting him with my crop, from time to time, *whack!,* between the flattened ears. Past Pete's Tavern. *Whoosh!* Past the chattering clusters of ladies and the sleeping dogs. Oh, they might complain about my walloping the shit out of the animal just to make good time—a galloping horse makes one hell of a lot of noise. Sounds like a war, actually. I wasn't doing it for speed, I'd tell the cops. I could not give a rat's ass if someone else held the record for racing a horse through Gramercy Park at night at a full gallop. And the cops would say, And, for our part, we don't give a rat's ass *why* you were doing it, mister. Fuck you and the horse you rode in on! So, I guess that answers my question.

In summer camp, one of the horses died in the middle of the night. The pinto dropped dead in his stall. They brought in buckets of lye for his burial. He had to be cut up into pieces so that they could fit him in his grave, which had to be deep. So they cut him into pieces, and they dug the grave. All this they did before dawn, so none of us kids saw any evidence of the dead pinto, except for the streaks of lye on the fresh earth. We did see that.

Did you know that in Hiroshima, the Bomb blasted the legs off horses? They stood, momentarily, with no legs. Hard to walk with no legs.

EASY ENOUGH TO say that you can be both a writer and a detective. A lot harder to pull it off. Sure, you can make up some easy explanation that both trades involve a searching for the truth, that both make use of research, that both require an appreciation of history, psychology, a knowledge of the patterns of human behavior, and so forth. You can add that the writer and the detective work on their own, that each knows a creative sort of loneliness, that their temperaments are similar—a mixture of toughness and childish optimism, of gruffness and a sense of play, of innocence and irony. A writer and a detective also learn to take rough treatment from the outer world, to take some hits, and to give as good as they get.

But, when you think about it, a detective builds his case on hard facts, ballistics and prints, types of weapons, eyewitnesses, people seen and heard here and there; on things that are real and really said. The fun in the TV series *Murder, She Wrote* was catching the inevitable slip of the tongue by the killer high up in the show, and then watching Jessica Fletcher, Angela Lansbury, nail the guilty party with it later on. The writer, on the other hand, builds his case from thin air. First he invents the crimes, then he manufactures the solutions. He may get as worked up about his mysteries as the detective does, but his mysteries never happened. I realize this business gets complicated when one is speaking of fictional detectives who are writers' creations. But once we start to read detective stories, the characters take on a life of their own, separated from the writers who gave birth to them. And while a writer may fancy himself a detective from time to time, not a single fictional professional detective has ever been a writer. Of course, sometimes the detective writes in the first person to tell his story, à la Philip Marlowe. But that is simply how the story gets to us. The writer is always a sidekick. Nero Wolfe had his Archie Goodwin, Vance had Van Dine, Holmes had Watson, whom he often accused of over-romanticizing his exploits.

Yet if you take the wider view, a writer and a detective may merge quite successfully, as each has what the other needs. The detective works principally with knowledge, the writer with feeling. And the most difficult cases are solved when these streams converge. George Eliot defined the poet's soul as "that which is equally quick to learn and quick to feel—a soul in which knowledge passes instantaneously into feeling and feeling flashes back as a new organ of knowledge." That's it, you see, and when both knowledge and feeling are applied in the service of the thing not seen, the thing imagined, not possible, such as the surprise identity of the criminal, well, then anything is possible.

The one thing they both require—the writer and the detective—is the desire to see what is not there, and to make it at once orderly and beautiful, as in a flower or the answer to a math problem. George C. Scott's Holmes saw the world only for what it could be. The sublime detective, the sublime writer.

AND EVEN WHEN you see a little, you never see the whole thing, any more than you can the whole room in which you sit

or the street on which you walk. There is always something
unseen above you or behind you. Just like the truth in a murder case. You never see the whole. Just like the city. Plaza by
plaza, esplanade by esplanade, you make your way in the discrete parts of the city the way you would travel the works of
a clock, each block an intricacy of gears and wheels. At first,
you wonder about the scope and shape of the entire entity, the
larger machine. Then you see that the parts are self-sufficient,
each park or square composed so that the residents might
feel some level of control and understanding about where
they live. No one lives in New York. Everyone lives on Tenth
Street, or on St. Marks Place, or in Gramercy Park.

Or in Tudor City, where my walk takes me now. Strangely
spiritless yet beautiful, the apartment house complex between
Fortieth and Forty-second streets and First Avenue once constituted the first residential skyscrapers in the world. A devel-
oper named Fred F. French had a vision of an urban utopia,
by way of Tudor England, which probably guaranteed his
disappointment. The area was more dangerous yet interesting as a slum known as Goat Hill in the 1850s, a home for
roving goats and gangs. French filled it with tulip gardens,
golf courses, and private playgrounds, all of which remain,
sans the golf course, in a kind of odorless splendor.

On a winter night, Tudor City feels no more lifeless than
it does on a summer day. Hard to know why. I walk in and out
as I did when I was a boy detective, no suspects in sight, with

no residual interest in the place except for the fact that my parents lived here before I was born. My mother described their Murphy bed, which disappeared into a wall. An innocent detail. My one noteworthy item about Tudor City.

WHAT DO YOU think, pal? Is there such a thing as an innocent detail? Apparent guilt means innocence, apparent innocence, guilt? It's nonsense, of course. But that's what Perry Mason was about, and Miss Marple and Nick Charles, and Charlie Chan, too. Holmes was made of subtler stuff. Assemble the sus*pects,* as Nick Charles pronounced the word, in one room. Scan the crowd from face to face. And the one who bears the blandest expression, who appears to have no reaction to the event, and seems to be present in the lineup merely as filler, he or she is the one. "*You* are murderer," says Charlie Chan to the least demonstrative of the lot.

I suppose it's the mystery writer's version of the appearance versus reality business taught in university literature courses. But it doesn't wash in life. In life, just as often, the guilty look guilty, the innocent look clean as a whistle, and everyone looks every possible way. In my own childhood pursuits of the killer, I never assumed that he would look anything but guilty, if he appeared to me at all. The light of hell in *They Might Be Giants.* In my many childhood wanderings, I could imagine something similar. Oddly, I could never foresee my bringing my criminal to justice or even taking him down in a shoot-out. But I could see myself facing him and finding my triumph in that moment of confrontation.

And I wondered what my quarry would find in that same moment. Would he look upon his adversary, his nemesis, and be afraid? Or would he assess me top to bottom, boy that I was, and conclude that I was as he always had imagined me? And would he have surprised me with a twist of plot and lashed out, "*You* are murderer"?

CAN YOU DIRECT me to the National Arts Club?

Can you direct me to the fish market?

Do you happen to know the location of the nearest public library?

Do you happen to know where a guy can get laid around here?

Where's a cop when you need one?

Am I going east or west? I'm going south?

Are you from here?

Do I know you?

YOURS IS THE clarity, the shape, and the theme. Mine is the shambles. And if I say that I am lost in admiration of

you, while that is true, it is truer that I am lost, period, lost
in everything. Nonetheless, I proceed even without a course
or destination. Without a firm location, I proceed. Are most
things nowhere? Stars, for instance. Isn't space the antithesis
of place? Or can an object be tethered to nothing? By what do
stars read their own positions?

But I probably am wrong in my premise. The "you" I
address who seems to have clarity, shape, and a theme is
more likely a fiction reserved for strangers. Or for people
one invents to look down on. No one has clarity, shape, and
a theme. The detective only has the lives of other people
under control. His own is in shambles, the very material
he draws on to solve his cases and close his books. Shambles. The headlights of cars fill your face, clear as rain. Do
I know you?

WHO DOES SHE remind me of, the one in the red-checkered
scarf, looking up at me now, startled, as if I were a car horn,
before trudging on in the cold? I know. I was giving a talk
in Washington at the Hay-Adams Hotel, on a piece I'd done
for the *New York Times Magazine*. And this young woman—
brown hair, soft voice, sad eyes that kept her beauty in the
background—walked up to say that her husband, who had
been killed somewhere, had been moved by something I had
written sometime, and that she had read whatever it was her-

self, and that it had helped her, somehow. But there was more to her than that, and more to the way we came together in the public room. And then there was someone else saying something else, and all at once she was borne away with the crowd, as if on a raft blown by the wind. And at the end of my talk, there was more chatter still, with strangers, and I had lost sight of her, until, outside the Hay-Adams, as my hired car started off, there she was again, standing in front of the others, looking directly through the car window at me. And what I might have done was to tell the driver to stop, to have flung open the car door, to have taken her small hand and pulled her inside, beside me, on that black leather seat, and asked her about her husband and her life.

Love at first sight? It wasn't that. There is no such thing as love at first sight, because it takes the imagination a while to dream up what love is. The one you catch sight of, on whom you have bestowed your sudden love, may be, at best, the perfect being revealed to you only after all the imperfect beings who preceded her. And if that is so, then love at first sight means love at last, the opposite of what it says. None of this applies to the one in the red-checkered scarf, since I have known my love-at-last since high school. Still, I might have spoken with her, so that we could have exchanged parts of our lives, in a world where daughters and husbands drop like flies. So that's who she reminds me of, the one in the red-checkered scarf.

CLEAVE ME INTO my parts and make me choose? I'd pick the heart over the head any day, because everybody is smart, you know, but not everybody is kind. That fellow with the lowered eyes, who sits in the frosted window of the print shop at Fortieth and Third, what words can I bring to ease his burden? None. Not a single intelligent word. But I could sit beside him on a stool and say nothing. That I could do. A tear is an intellectual thing, said Blake.

The thing about John Lewis playing Bach, you see, is that his right hand plays Bach straight, as it's written, and his left hand plays jazz and does the improvising. You might say that his left hand lives in the moment, and his right hand in the past. You get the allusion? Hear what I mean? Or, am I beating a dead horse?

I'D SAY WE were nearing the end of our illimitable walk, but as you know, that cannot be. I may be near the end of my personal walk, but that's a smaller matter. So let's just say that I am at Fifty-first and Lex, which is a bit north of my range. I am here nonetheless, because the Loew's Lexington movie theater used to be here, with its pool of glittering goldfish in the center of the lobby. Neighborhood kids passed whole Saturdays at the Loew's. We were herded into the children's section patrolled by "matrons" with white uniforms and great thick hands, and we watched a double feature of A and B movies, short subjects, such as the Pete Smith comedies, the glorious cartoons of Chuck Jones, and Movietone News. We would arrive at the theater at ten in the morning, cough up our twenty-five cents for admission, and be out no earlier than four in the afternoon.

It was here that I saw the noir film *Shadow on the Wall*, which presented a lesson on how to make use of confusing information in a murder case and elsewhere. *Shadow on the Wall* was about a girl my age, eight or nine, and I saw it at the time I was sleeping in my parents' bedroom and was watching shadows on the ceiling. The little girl witnesses a murder committed by a woman who killed her sister in a jealous rage. The murderess wore a hat with a prominent feather. So traumatized is the little girl that she temporarily loses her memory, and all she can tell the police is that the murderer was an Indian. The murderer, knowing that the girl's memory will return, plans to kill her.

Down the length of Lexington Avenue we kids would walk in the late afternoons dueling with invisible swords if the movie we had just seen was *Scaramouche*, or howling through the jungle, if the movie was *Tarzan*. Past the place that sold candy apples and caramel apples. Past the Army, Navy and Marines Club, twin gray town houses with American flags sticking out on poles. Past Joe's Photo Shop on Twenty-fourth, where I had my first job, at age eleven, sweeping out the store on early Saturday mornings and earn-ing two dollars, so that I had a fortune to take to the movies. Past the George Washington Hotel, where I got haircuts and smelled of witch hazel. Then down to Gramercy Park, where Lexington Avenue ends or begins, depending on one's perspective.

Traffic moved two ways on Lex in those days. When the one-way change was instituted, and all the cars moved south toward the park, drivers at night would often build up a head of steam, hurtle down the avenue, and plough into the Gramercy Park gate. Awakened, I would hear them yell, "Who put this park here!" A conversation-stopper, in case you run out: Lexington Avenue was the site of the first speeding ticket issued in New York, in 1899. A cabdriver was pulled over for going twelve miles an hour.

The avenue, so important to us kids, is not known for much history. An anarchist bombing occurred here in 1914. And a few years ago, there was an explosion at Forty-first Street, when a geyser of steam scalded dozens of pedestrians. To anyone who has seen *The Seven Year Itch,* Lexington Avenue is where Marilyn Monroe stood over an IRT subway grate in front of the Loew's Lexington movie theater, her white skirt billowing up to heaven.

Down from Fifty-first Street again tonight, walking toward Gramercy Park. The avenue funnels bright before me like the barrel of a gun, and the winter sky turns purple. From *Shadow on the Wall* a detective learns that when faced with information that makes no sense yet comes from a reliable source, you need to imagine an explanation. Take a leap. When you have eliminated the impossible, what remains, however improbable, must be the truth. Don't look for the Indian. Look for the feather.

SOMETHING FAULKNER SAID in *Light in August*: "Memory believes before knowing remembers. Believes longer than recollects, longer than knowing even wonders." He seems to think of memory as a kind of faith. And he is proved right, if we dredge up old Jay Gatsby, believing with all his might in the past as he attempts to re-create it. And Daisy, the worthless object of desire, the flimsy embodiment of the past herself, could not care less. Yet Gatsby keeps the faith.

So, does this mean that a memoir is an act of faith, and that the various worlds we write into creation represent our way of making a heaven and a church—all the things that receive belief? A god itself? We might ask ourselves why this form of writing exists. And the answer may be that the memoir is an instrument by which we redo our lives in order to have something to believe in. As unhappy or confused as our memories may be—as chilling or terrifying or just plain sad—the accretion of them, nonetheless, becomes a kind of altar at which we worship. The structure constitutes our salvation. Quasimodo cries out to the cathedral of Notre Dame, If only

I were made out of stone like thee. The church, our Lady of Memory, becomes our sanctuary.

Which is to say, students, your memoir is not about you. So, stay out of it. Keep clear of your memoir, except in those instances where your idiosyncratic, weird, freakish life speaks for others, for all lives. As you write, let your mind wander, for wandering is necessary for your memoir. Let your mind wander to subjects outside your worries, shames, griefs, and traumas—no matter how devastating or exciting they may be—to history, plain facts, abstract thoughts, and to the people for whom you write. At the outset of a memoir, you are propelled by the desire to let the world know who you are. Soon you will discover that you don't really care that much about who you are, and that writing with that goal alone will turn boring, cloying. You will tire of yourself just as you tire of others who think only of themselves, and whose chatterings are mere perseverations of autobiography.

I'll say it again. Your life is not about you. Or to put it more usefully, it is about the you in you that is common to everyone. Your life is about everyone. In his tender *Autobiography,* the poet Edwin Muir describes his emotional awakening after undergoing psychoanalysis for the first time. "I saw that my lot was the human lot," he writes. And "in my own unvarnished likeness, I was one among all men and women." To see that is not only to acknowledge something essential about one's life. It also serves the writing of the memoir by diverting the reader's attention from the one to the many, while at the same time, the one uses the many to try to discover who the one really is and what his story is about. Your memoir is not about you. You are the world in which you walk, you and everyone else, to boot.

"THIS IS WHERE Daddy was born," says Ginny with a sweep of her arm. Our three children inspect Gramercy Park as if they might uncover mementos of my birth. Arrowheads. Here memory recalls memory. The scene is a floral print. I feel powerful and useless in my stride, the way the giants of fairy tales must feel when they encounter heroes of normal size. The gravel crunches under our feet. Soon it is Verdun, and I am trying to rush ahead of Ginny and the kids in order to take the first volley of shells. Bullets fly like apples. I am shouting, "Down! Get down!" Then it is spring again. Everyone is okay.

WHAT IF WE thought of time not as a measurement and not as an abstraction, but rather as a place—a city, for instance, or a part of a city, or a park—a place you can leave yet never leave? In your mind, of course. We are speaking of your mind. Yet this city, or part of a city, or park, does nothing to you, the way time, normally defined, can. And you can do nothing to it, the way you can waste time, normally defined, or kill it. Time seen as a place simply serves you as a permanent point of reference. And, like any old place, there are good things associated with it, and bad. But neither good nor bad, happy thoughts or unhappy thoughts, or feelings of anxiety or serenity or any feeling at all has the slightest effect on the fact that this is your place in the world. Period. Here you stand, or walk. And here you wait to see whatever will happen to you, which turns out to be the very thing that is happening to you as you stand, or walk.

So, if you buy the hypothesis, this is your place of time. It is here that you recognize yourself, however dimly, and here that you steady yourself when need be, and regroup. The where is the when. And if you should happen to wear a wristwatch in the where, the watch's face would show neither hands nor numbers, but rather trees, shops, even yourself, your image. What? Do you think the world would be worse off if this were so? If you put your mind to it, could you not intuit a train schedule, or the minutes it takes to cook an egg? If you put your mind to it, whenever someone asked you the time, could you not look at your wrist and answer, "My home. My silent home"?

AFTER WEEKEND PERFORMANCES, I would head downtown to visit my mother in the Bialystoker Nursing Home on the Lower East Side, not far from Hester Street, where she used to teach. The performances were of a one-man show I wrote in 1991, called *Free Speech in America,* at the American Place Theatre. Some great plays were put on at the American Place, directed by its founder, Wynn Handman, such as William Alfred's *Hogan's Goat* and Robert Lowell's *The Old Glory.* Mine was hardly in that category. Yet it got a rave from the *New York Times,* thus what I expected to be a three-week run turned into a small hit that ran six months. Not being an actor, I ran out of steam and finally called a halt to it. I was spending as much on cab fare to and from the theater as I was making for the play. You know what they say: "You can make a killing in the theater, but not a living."

By then, my mother lived in the impenetrable darkness of Alzheimer's. The Bialystoker home was not fancy but clean and efficiently run, and the nurses were attentive. The floors were linoleum and the walls too brightly lit. The home smelled of soap and old people, who lay in beds not far from one another, separated by screens. A belligerent little woman used to roll nonstop through the aisles in her wheelchair at ridiculous speeds, cursing and complaining, her small hard face like a boxing jab. My mother rarely spoke. Once she mentioned that Mr. Homer had made a pass at her and had wanted to marry her after my father died. She smiled saying that. There was a two-week interval in which she was lucid, so much so that Ginny and I asked the doctor if my mother was actually getting better. He said such spasms of clarity were normal, and that she would slide back to the unreachable country, and she did. She usually recognized me, but often she would just smile or stare. Whenever Peter and Ginny joined me, she looked as if she knew us. Most of the time when I sat alone beside her bed, we maintained the silence that was familiar to us both.

ASSUMING THAT YOUR head has cleared in death, Mother, could you possibly spare a few minutes? I'd like to tell you something I've learned from a lifetime of detective work. I promise not to ask unseemly questions. You would not be accused. You would not be put on trial to explain yourself (as if that were possible for any of us). The maple leaves would rise and fall around us—say we were sitting on a park bench, one of the benches with commemorative plaques. Sparrows would peek out of their little holes in the birdhouse. At other benches, the Gramercy women would be speaking of Switzerland and the Catholic Church. Your cronies at the Marshall Chess Club would be on hand if you should need them, and your mother, too, and Patta, and your sister Julia, perhaps even Peter and Dad. And there would be other people, sights and sounds you are comfortable with, so you would have no cause for anxiety. Then, when you were at ease and assured that all was safe, and that I meant well, I would tell you, after

a long embrace, and though I did not mean it, that I no longer
wish to be right.

ROUND AND ROUND the park. Round and round. My favorite part of being a detective is just this—the walk, just taking
in the world. Soon enough someone will engage us on a hunt,
a project. And off we will go, armed to the hilt with whatever
powers we possess, of reason, deduction, and style. We shall
put our powers to use for the sake of honor, decency, and justice. And that's all to the good, just as it should be in a life that
yearns for honor, decency, and justice.

But before all that, and afterward, too, life calls for nothing but itself. And we do not so much pursue it as let it wrap
around us, and just as quickly, unwrap, like the wind. Now
that I think about it, the reason I sat at the kitchen window
working on the sill day after day may have had less to do with
the digging than with what it had avoided. The dog that did
not bark. The digging into the marble sill may simply have
been a diversion from the world I saw whenever I looked
up. My view. And I was so overwhelmed with what lay before me, the grand endless mystery that opened before me,
that I averted my gaze for fear of being blinded. For past the
window lay the city, and the pitch of the rooftops, and the
pulse of the clouds, and the black water tanks, and the trees
reaching up and the people reaching up, and everyone and

everything murmuring in a silent chorus, "We're alive." I felt that myself. "I'm alive." And I may have realized, in the hidden way that children realize things, that the idea of life, wondrous life, was stronger and more durable than any assaults, loud or silent, that of all the gifts my world afforded whenever I walked out into it, the most terrifying and miraculous was this announcement, "I'm alive," enforced with every step.

How do you walk in the world? That's no trick. The *how* is easy. Or if it is not always easy, it is at least clear. How to walk in the world? Walk as the private eye walks. Do right, play fair, ignore the trash, and keep your nose clean. But *why* does one walk in the world? That's another matter. Which brings me to you, as ever, and you to me. Will you be my partner? Shall we do our walking side by side? What do you say? See? I wasn't tracking you, after all—through the fog and the screams and the gunshots. I might have thought I was tracking you. But all I ever wanted was to face you, in the blessed, blazing light.

And now it is past midnight. And the park is visible only in contours, ghost-trees that menace us no longer. I am alone no longer, and neither are you. So why do we walk in the world? The pitch of the rooftops, and the pulse of the clouds, and the black water tanks, and the trees reaching up and the people reaching up. And you, pal. Guilty, blameless you.

ACKNOWLEDGMENTS

Many thanks to Ginny Rosenblatt, Dan Halpern, Jane Freeman, Libby Edelson, Gloria Loomis, Leon Wieseltier, Julia Masnik, Lou Ann Walker, David Lynn, and Kay Allaire.